VOLCANOES
IN AMERICA'S NATIONAL PARKS

BY ROBERT DECKER AND BARBARA DECKER

VOLCANOES
IN AMERICA'S NATIONAL PARKS

BY ROBERT DECKER AND BARBARA DECKER

Volcanoes in America's National Parks

Copyright © 2001 Airphoto International Ltd.
Maps Copyright © 2001 Airphoto International Ltd.

Airphoto International Ltd., 903 Seaview Commercial Building,
21-24 Connaught Road West, Sheung Wan, Hong Kong
Tel: (852) 2856-3896; Fax: (852) 2565-8004; E-mail: odyssey@asiaonline.net

**Distributed in the United States of America by
WW Norton & Company Inc.
500 Fifth Avenue, New York, NY 10110, USA
Tel: 800-233-4830; Fax: 800-458-6515
World Wide Web: www.wwnorton.com**

ISBN: 962-217-677-1

Edited by Barry Parr.
Designed by Leslie Wilks, singlespace design studio, St. Helena, California.
Maps by Mark Stroud, Moon Street Cartography, Durango, Colorado.

Photography by Bob Decker and Barbara Decker unless otherwise noted.
Front cover and frontispiece: Mount Rainier by George Wuerthner.
Back cover: Kilauea Volcano arching lava fountain by J.D. Griggs, USGS;
Castle Geyser by Don Pitcher.

Production by Twin Age Ltd.
1401 Chung Ying Building,
20-20A Connaught Road West,
Sheung Wan, Hong Kong
E-mail: twinage@netvigator.com

Manufactured in China.

VOLCANOES IN AMERICA'S NATIONAL PARKS

CONTENTS

PREFACE

If you had to guess how many of America's national parks and monuments have volcanoes as their central theme, or in a major supporting role, how many would you say? Ten? Twenty? Thirty?

The answer is at least 38; 20 where volcanoes are the main theme, and 18 or more where volcanoes have major supporting roles. We have been interested in volcanoes for many years, but this large number surprised even us. After thinking about it, we can see three main reasons why volcanoes are the stars, or major supporting players, of so many places in America's national park system.

First, volcanic eruptions are rare, awesome and fascinating. They are symbolic of the power of nature. Thirty-five volcanoes in the United States have erupted one or more times during the 20th century: Kilauea and Mauna Loa in Hawaii, Mount St. Helens in Washington State, Lassen Peak in California, and 31 others in Alaska, including Katmai, whose eruption in 1912 was the largest in the world in the 20th century. All four of the volcanoes that have erupted since AD 1900 in Hawaii, Washington, and California—and six more in Alaska—are in national parks or monuments.

Sleeping volcanoes that have erupted during the past 100,000 years but not during the 20th century number somewhere between 100 and 200 in the United States, depending on who is counting. Many of these dormant volcanoes, for example Haleakala on the Island of Maui, are also in national parks. Going way back in time, about a 100 million years, what are now the granite domes and cliffs of Yosemite were once chambers of molten rock feeding a chain of volcanoes that have long since eroded away. We list this variety of volcanic park in Part Four, "Ancient Fires."

The second reason is that volcanoes, erupting or sleeping, are beautiful and majestic mountains, and are often in pristine areas where there has been little or no human disturbance to the native forests and wildlife. They are sanctuaries of the way the world was. Mount Rainier National Park, next door to the city of Seattle, is a good example of this category.

Thirdly, unique thermal features like the world-famous geysers of Yellowstone National Park in Wyoming, and the wild and wonderful volcanic rock outcrops in Arizona's Chiricahua National Monument are rare and fascinating natural wonders.

The part called "Mountains of Fire" is a brief introduction to the science of volcanoes—where they occur and how they work. It provides a background for understanding the descriptions of volcanoes in individual parks and monuments in parts Two, Three and Four, which then can be read in any order depending on your interest or travel plans.

The national park system uses many designations for its units—National Park, National Monument, National Preserve, and so on. While we use the correct name for each specific unit, when we refer to these wonderful places as a group, for simplicity's sake we call them parks. All the places we write about are in the national park system, but Mount St. Helens National Volcanic Monument, Newberry National Volcanic Monument and Giant Sequoia National Monument are administered by the U.S. Forest Service.

Our book is centered on volcanoes, but each place we write about is rich in other wonders—history, scenery, wild flora and fauna. If we tried to describe it all you wouldn't be able to lift this book. We hope you'll go see the volcanoes, and discover each park's other treasures for yourself.

Volcanoes have their roots deep below the surface, and blast their ashes high into the sky. Discovering how they work helps us understand our dynamic Earth, and seeing and studying them in our national parks is both an education and a delight.

Bob and Barbara Decker, Kawaihae, Hawaii, 2001

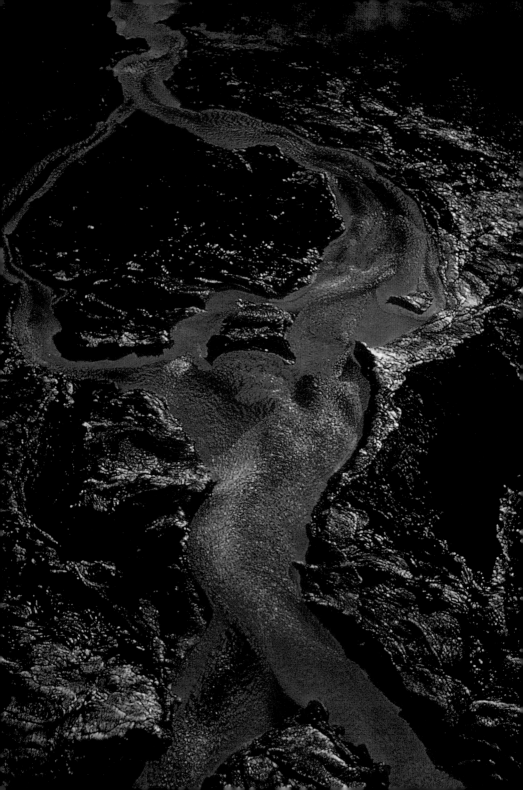

Part One

MOUNTAINS OF FIRE

Pele, the Hawaiian Goddess of Volcanoes, makes her home in Hawaii Volcanoes National Park. She commands the eruptions—where and when they happen, how big they are, and how long they last. Legend says she can travel from her home at the summit of Kilauea Volcano by a road underground, to pour forth red hot lava at vents on the side of the mountain. She stamps her foot to make earthquakes and chases lesser gods through the forest with her consuming fires. Pele is central to the legends that explain the creation of the Hawaiian island chain and the features of its volcanic landscape. She directs the mystery of how Hawaiian volcanoes work.

Mount St. Helens, in legend, was called Loowit, Lady of Fire. Sometimes an ugly witch and at other times a beautiful woman, she was not only the goddess of the mountain, she *was* the mountain. Violent eruptions revealed the witch, and time renewed the beauty.

At Crater Lake, Llao, Chief of the Below World, and his arch enemy Skell, Chief of the Upper World, fought a great battle. Skell tore Llao apart, throwing his pieces into the huge crater. Tears from Llao's mourners filled the crater with its clear blue lake.

In a way all these myths and legends tell something real about the origin of these magnificent volcanoes from the time when history was passed from generation to generation by storytelling. Little wonder that the great powers of nature were feared or revered as gods and goddesses. Science has stripped some of the mystery from these awesome mountains, but they still retain mysteries aplenty.

What is a volcano? The word volcano is used to describe either a mountain built up of volcanic rock, or a vent that pours out molten rock and volcanic ashes. The definition depends on the way the word is used. For example, Mount Rainier Volcano towers over the city of Seattle. Used this way "volcano" refers to the great mountain of lava and ash built up over hundreds of thousands of years by thousands of eruptions.

In another example, Kilauea Volcano in Hawaii has been erupting molten lava almost continuously since 1983, and still is in 2001. Used this way "volcano" refers to the vents from which molten rock and volcanic gases escape from deep within the Earth to the surface. Since Kilauea Volcano has had many different vents over the past thousands of years, individual eruptions and vents are often given more specific names such as the Pu'u O'o vent, the site of the current eruption.

Giving something a name is only part of the story. The next questions are where do volcanoes occur, and why do they form at these locations?

While photographing lava streams flowing down Hawaii's Mauna Loa Volcano, Katia Krafft captured this dramatic image which she named "Pele Dancing," to honor the Hawaiian goddess of volcanoes.

THE RESTLESS EARTH

▼ **Below:** *Dots indicate locations of earthquakes greater than magnitude 4.5 during a period of 14 years. Heavy concentrations are along subduction and strike-slip zones; lighter lines mark rift zones.*

More than 200 years ago Benjamin Franklin pointed out that the shapes of Africa and South America were like jigsaw puzzle pieces that could fit together into one larger continent. Early in the 20th century, a German scientist named Alfred Wegener took this idea a major step forward. He showed that not only could the shapes of Africa and South America be fit together, but that the geologic pattern of both continents was continuous. In other words not only did the blank jigsaw puzzle pieces fit together, but the broken pictures on both pieces also matched. Wegener called his theory continental drift.

The major problem with continental drift was that Wegener and his allies could not propose a reasonable explanation of the forces that drove the continental fragments apart. His opponents, world renowned geophysicists, argued that the upper layers of the Earth were too strong to permit the movement of continents. Until the 1950s continental drift remained an interesting but discredited idea.

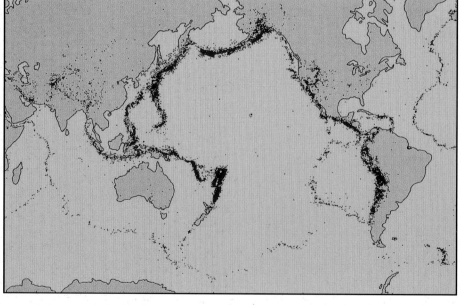

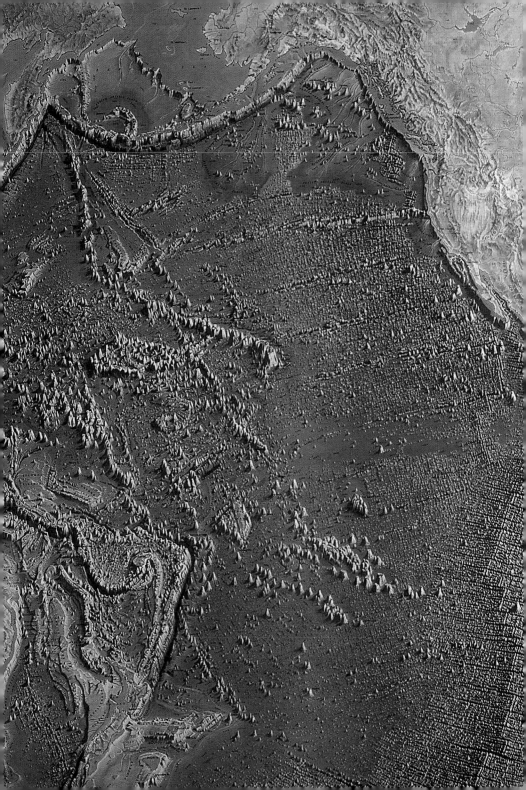

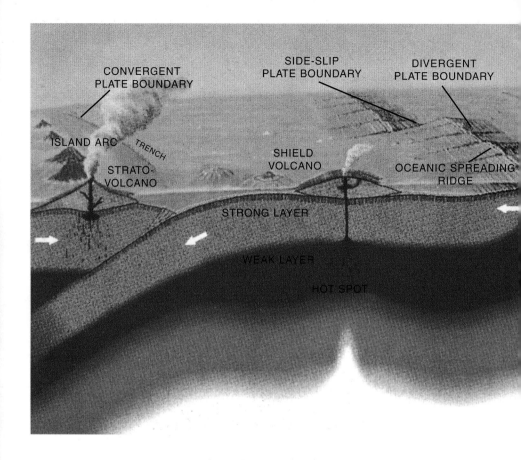

CONVERGENT PLATE BOUNDARY

SIDE-SLIP PLATE BOUNDARY

DIVERGENT PLATE BOUNDARY

ISLAND ARC

TRENCH

STRATO-VOLCANO

SHIELD VOLCANO

OCEANIC SPREADING RIDGE

STRONG LAYER

WEAK LAYER

HOT SPOT

▲ *Diagram of how geologists imagine a 300-mile-deep slice into the Earth might appear. The tectonic plates move slowly on a layer of hot, low-strength rocks in the Earth's upper mantle. Although the surface features in this diagram are schematic, the convergent plate boundary on the left could represent Japan, the shield volcano above the hot spot the Island of Hawaii, and the divergent plate boundary the East Pacific Rise.*
(Continued on opposite page.)

During the 1960s the theory resurfaced, but with a new twist. Scientists who were studying the seafloor discovered that the rocks beneath the oceans were largely very young lava flows along the crests of the mid-ocean ridges, but progressively older on both sides of the ridges. They called the idea seafloor spreading. Instead of Africa and South America actively drifting away from one another by moving through the oceanic crust, the oceanic crust itself was spreading slowly at the Mid-Atlantic Ridge and carrying the continental fragments away from one another like two ships locked into the separate parts of a spreading ice floe. The idea quickly took hold, but two major hurdles remained: If some seafloors were spreading, was the Earth expanding, or was the crust in some other places converging? Also, what about the objections that the Earth's upper layers were too strong to permit drift or spreading?

Zones where the huge plates of the Earth's crust converge were soon identified. These places, generally related to deep sea trenches and inclined zones of earthquake locations, were named

　　　MOUNTAINS OF FIRE

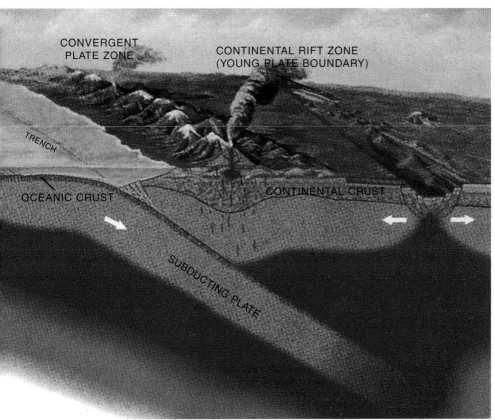

CONVERGENT
PLATE ZONE

CONTINENTAL RIFT ZONE
(YOUNG PLATE BOUNDARY)

TRENCH

OCEANIC CRUST

CONTINENTAL CRUST

SUBDUCTING PLATE

Modified from Jose Vigil, U.S. Geological Survey

subduction zones. At these places the edge of one of Earth's plates plunges beneath another. Most often the plunging edge—if you can call a few inches per year "plunging"—is seafloor, and the overriding edge continental.

As the major plates of the Earth's crust and their motions relative to one another have been identified, the concept has become known as plate tectonics. The word tectonics as used by geologists refers to the structure and dynamics of large scale features of the Earth. Instead of being rejected like Wegener's original idea of continental drift, plate tectonics has become the major unifying theory of geology.

Present investigations into plate tectonics largely concern the mechanisms that drive the plate motions. Some scientists favor push-apart forces at the mid-ocean ridges where the plates are diverging; others think the plunging edges of plates are pulled down by their own increasing density at subduction zones; and still others consider that convection currents—slow stirrings in the Earth's hot, solid but plastic mantle—drag the plates along from below.

The convergent plate zone could represent the Cascade volcanoes in northwest United States, and the continental rift zone could represent Owens Valley and Death Valley in California.

Push, pull, or drag? Perhaps all three forces are at work in different parts of the world. Often the more a process is studied the more complex it appears.

Seismologists—scientists who study earthquakes and the vibrational waves they generate—were the ones who originally objected to Wegener's continental drift idea. Their analyses of earthquake waves passing through the Earth revealed a molten core surrounded by a thick mantle of hot but solid rock as strong as steel. Taking a closer look in the 1960s, and using details from the earthquake waves generated by nuclear bomb tests, a new generation of seismologists discovered a layer of low strength about 100 miles below the Earth's surface. Apparently composed of partly-molten rock, this layer marks the bottom of the tectonic plates and provides the weak zone on which the plates can move.

And the plates do move, but at velocities that make glaciers look like speed demons. A few inches per year, or about as fast as fingernails grow, are common descriptions of the speed of tectonic plate motions. Nevertheless, these cumulative motions add up over geologic time scales. The Atlantic Ocean has opened over 200

▼ *Map of the Earth's tectonic plates. Arrows indicate the slow plate-motion directions relative to adjacent plates. The rates of plate motion vary from about four inches per year (the Pacific plate) to less than one inch per year.*

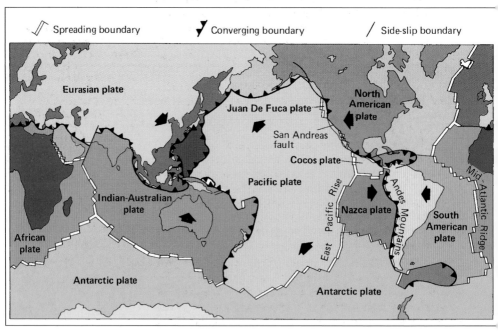

Spreading boundary   Converging boundary   Side-slip boundary

Eurasian plate

Juan De Fuca plate

North American plate

San Andreas fault

Cocos plate

Pacific plate

Indian-Australian plate

African plate

Nazca plate

South American plate

Andes Mountains

East Pacific Rise

Mid-Atlantic Ridge

Antarctic plate

Antarctic plate

Modified from Warren Hamilton U.S. Geological Survey

MOUNTAINS OF FIRE

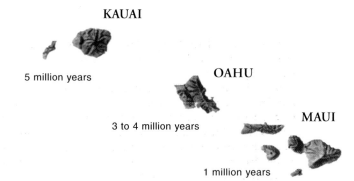

KAUAI

5 million years

OAHU

3 to 4 million years

MAUI

1 million years

HAWAII

0 to 1/2 million years

million years, and California's San Andreas Fault has slipped nearly 20 miles over the past million years.

The slow motions of the plates build up large stresses and strains, particularly along the plate edges. Earthquakes periodically relieve these stresses. The breaking edges of the plates are earthquake country—Japan, where plates converge, Iceland, where plates diverge, and California, where plates suddenly slip sideways along the notorious San Andreas Fault.

Earthquake country is often volcano country as well, a relationship sometimes called the "creaking and leaking edges" of the plates. Most of the diverging or rifting plate edges are mid-ocean ridges, where submarine volcanoes are apparently common but obviously difficult to study. In the few places where diverging plate edges occur on land, like Iceland and the Rift Valleys of East Africa, rift volcanoes are numerous.

The other major homes of volcanoes are the subduction zones where the plates converge. Subduction volcanoes form the Ring of Fire around the Pacific Rim, where many plates are converging on the Pacific plate. The volcanoes of Alaska, Washington, Oregon and Northern California belong to this subduction variety. Most of the live volcanoes discussed in this book—Mount St. Helens, Lassen, Aniakchak, Katmai, Novarupta, Redoubt, and Wrangell—are subduction volcanoes that erupted during the 20th century.

A third major class of volcanoes occurs at hot spots, often far removed from the edges of the tectonic plates. This family of volcanoes has helped to confirm the fact that the plates are moving. For example, the Hawaiian Hot Spot, named by Canadian geophysicist Tuzo Wilson in 1963, has been generating volcanoes for tens of millions of years. The live volcanoes Kilauea and Mauna Loa in Hawaii

▲ *The Hawaiian Islands were built (and are still being built) by volcanoes that once grew (and are still growing) over the Hawaiian Hot Spot. The approximate ages of their lavas as shown on the map are progressively older away from the Island of Hawaii. The age of an island and its distance from the hot spot indicate the direction and rate of motion of the Pacific plate–about four inches per year to the west northwest.*

Data from the U.S. Geological Survey.

Jerry Eaton, USGS

▲ *Fiery spatter cone on the East Rift of Kilauea Volcano, Hawaii. During rift zone eruptions lava may travel many miles underground in deep fractures, called dikes, that extend from the summit magma chamber beneath Kilauea to the eruption site.*

Volcanoes National Park now lie directly above the hot spot. Wilson argued that as the Pacific Plate moves northwest over a relatively fixed hot spot, older and eventually dead volcanoes would form a chain of islands that have moved away from their hot-spot source. Other evidence indicates the Pacific Plate is moving to the northwest at about four inches per year. Wilson predicted that if his hot-spot idea was the correct hypothesis for the origin of the Hawaiian Islands, the ancient lava flows that form Maui, Oahu, and Kauai would turn out to be progressively older by about 1.6 million years for each 100 miles they have moved away from their origin at the hot spot (100 miles divided by 4 inches per year equals 1,584,000 years). Radiometric dating of lava from the older Hawaiian islands has confirmed Wilson's bold prediction. Kauai, 325 miles northwest of Mauna Loa, is about 5.1 million years old; Oahu, 220 miles northwest, is 2.6 to 3.7 million years old; and Maui, 100 miles northwest, is 0.7 to 1.3 million years old. The oldest rocks dated on the Island of Hawaii, present home of the hot spot, are less than 0.5 million years old, and some have just been born.

Hot-spot volcanoes, although not directly related to the edges of plates, may cause some of the slow stirrings in the Earth's mantle that are thought to drive the plates. In this idea, plumes of hot plastic rock moving slowly upward, considered to be the roots of hot spots, are deflected sideways beneath the rigid plates.

The close relationship between volcanoes and plate tectonics is clear. Most of them occur at or near the plate edges, and hot-spot volcanoes may be caused by slow-moving plumes of hot plastic rock deep within the Earth that help propel the plates.

Heat stirs the restless Earth. Although it is much less than the heat from the sun, the heat from inside the Earth fires the volcanoes and moves the plates. What is the origin of this heat? Some of it is leftover heat from the formation of the Earth and its molten core billions of years ago. If there were no other ongoing source of heat generation, however, the present rate of heat loss through the Earth's

▼ *Shattered summit of the stratovolcano Mount St. Helens after its 1980 explosive eruption. Mount St. Helens is one of 15 major volcanoes along the Cascade Subduction Zone. The summit of Mount St. Helens before the 1980 eruption was 9,677 feet high. After the eruption the high point on the crater rim is only 8,365 feet.*

Lyn Topinka, U.S. Geological Survey

▲ View of Mount St. Helens from Spirit Lake in 1963. This beautifully symmetrical stratovolcano was named by the British navy explorer George Vancouver in 1792 to honor Baron St. Helens, a British nobleman. Earthquakes and small explosive eruptions beginning in late March 1980 brought more than a century of tranquillity on this volcano to an end.

surface would have chilled the interior eons ago. Most geophysicists agree that the major ongoing source of heat is the radioactive decay of uranium, thorium and potassium isotopes. Although these isotopes are very minor constituents of the Earth, and they break down and release heat very slowly, the great insulating quality of the massive Earth and the great length of geologic time combine to generate from these tiny heaters temperatures high enough to melt rocks. Imagine putting on enough warm clothes so that little or no heat escaped from your body. Even without exercise, your body temperature would slowly rise to levels high enough to kill you. Before this happens you pull off some clothes. In an analogous way, volcanoes help to vent the heat buildup inside the Earth.

It takes millions of years for radioactive heat to partially melt the low-strength layer beneath the plates. If that partial melt could collect into fully molten blobs of magma (molten rock with dissolved gases) that were less dense than the overlying rocks, the blobs would rise and volcanoes would be scattered randomly over the Earth's surface. Because they are not, other processes must be at work.

Two important principles besides heat are involved in the creation of molten rock. Rock under high pressure has a higher melting temperature than it would under lower pressure, so if very hot plastic rock moves upward into areas of lower pressure some of it will melt. The most common composition of that melt fraction is called basalt, a silicate melt roughly similar to molten brown glass with a silica (SiO_2) content of about 50 percent. At the margins of diverging plates, a mush of hot plastic rock moves upward to fill the space created by the separating plates. Basaltic magma is formed, and basalt dikes (cracks filled with magma) and surface eruptions fill the upper parts of the newly created space.

▼ *Climactic eruption of Mount St. Helens, on May 18, 1980. After a two-month buildup of small explosions, a giant landslide swept away the north side of the volcano. The sudden reduction in pressure on the magma beneath the mountain unleashed the great explosion.*

Robert Krimmel, USGS

▲ *Molten lava fountaining from the Pu'u O'o vent of Kilauea Volcano builds this growing, 200-foot-high cinder and spatter cone. Most volcanic eruptions in Hawaii are effusive rather than explosive; that is, they pour out fountains or streams of red-hot molten lava instead of the gray, hot but solid volcanic fragments expelled by explosive eruptions like Mount St. Helens.*

Once magma is erupted and loses most of its dissolved gas content, it is called lava. Volcanic eruptions are often intermittent because the rate of eruption of lava is generally, but not always, faster than the rate of magma supply from depth.

Hot-spot volcanoes that create oceanic islands are another example of magma generated by pressure reduction. As a plume of slightly hotter and therefore less-dense rock rises slowly upward through the Earth's mantle, part of the plume's top melts into basaltic magma. The molten basalt, lighter than the upper mantle and crustal rocks surrounding it, rises through fractures toward the surface to eventually erupt in volcanoes like Kilauea and Mauna Loa in Hawaii.

Another way in which additional magma is created involves the addition of water and carbon dioxide to the low-strength layer in the Earth's upper mantle. The subduction process accomplishes this by dragging down seafloor sediments on the top of the subducting plate in a manner similar to a very slow conveyor belt moving into the hot zone beneath the upper plate. Water-soaked sediments and shells of organisms composed of calcium carbonate release water and carbon dioxide as they are cooked by the heat in this hot zone. Water and carbon dioxide act as fluxes and lower the melting temperature of basaltic magma. Again, not all the hot rock melts since it takes energy to form the molten magma. At a depth of about 100 miles below the surface enough new molten basalt is generated to form the deep roots of subduction volcanoes.

Heat from radioactive isotopes is the basic energy that fuels the Earth's internal furnace, and the motions of the plates provide the reduction in pressure or the addition of water that help create the supply of basaltic magma that fires the Earth's volcanoes. In rift and hot-spot volcanoes it is largely pressure reduction, and in subduction volcanoes it is largely the fluxing action of water. Firefighters use water to put fires out; nature uses water to help melt rocks. The common-sense rules that apply at the Earth's surface are not always the same deep underground.

▼ *"Black Smokers," the nickname applied to submarine hot springs that emit dark clouds of metallic sulfide particles, are formed along mid-ocean ridges. This photo was taken from a French submersible at a depth of 8,000 feet along the East Pacific Rise.*

J. L. Cheminée, Observatoires Volcanologiques, Institut de Physique du Globe de Paris

VOLCANOES DEAD OR ALIVE

The habits of volcanoes are almost as peculiar and individual as those of human beings, so it is not unusual that geologists have borrowed some human terms to describe the behavior of volcanoes: active, live, sleeping or dormant, dead or extinct. Outraged humans may also erupt, but generally "erupting" is a volcanic adjective.

Erupting is obvious; an erupting volcano assails your senses. If you are nearby, you can see rivers of lava or clouds of ashes, hear hissing, roaring or explosions, smell and taste the sulfur gases, and feel the heat. An eruption may last for minutes or years, but witnessing one is an unforgettable experience whatever its duration.

An active volcano is one that is erupting or has erupted recently. But how long ago is "recently?" The International Association of Volcanology defines an active volcano as one that has erupted during recorded history. The problem with this definition is that the span of recorded history is much longer in some regions of the world than in others—more than 2,000 years in the Mediterranean and less than 250 years in Hawaii. The Smithsonian Institution defines a potentially active volcano as one that has erupted during the past 10,000 years. If you use recorded history there are about 600 active volcanoes in the world. Using the 10,000-year time span, the number grows to more than 1,500 active volcanoes.

For simplicity, we will use the terms erupting, live, asleep, and dead. An erupting volcano is one that is currently spewing out molten lava or volcanic ashes. Any volcano that has erupted since the beginning of the 20th century we will call a live volcano. A sleeping or dormant volcano is one that is not presently erupting but is likely to erupt again. Note that by these definitions, a volcano can be alive, yet sleeping. All the Smithsonian's list of potentially active volcanoes that are not currently erupting fall into the sleeping category. It is not unreasonable that a volcano with a million-year life span might sleep for 100,000 years between eruptions.

A dead or extinct volcano is one that will not erupt again. To be sure that the ancient fires of a volcano will not flare up again, it is wise to

▼ Pu'u O'o, the present vent of Kilauea Volcano in Hawaii, has been erupting since 1983. It is one of the world's best examples of a volcano that can be classified as both "active" and "live." Lava from Pu'u O'o and a nearby vent have flowed for years into the sea, adding new land to the Island of Hawaii.

J.D. Griggs, USGS

MOUNTAINS OF FIRE

look way back in geologic time. For example, the chambers that once held molten rock 100 million years ago beneath a great chain of subduction volcanoes along the crest of what is now the Sierra Nevada in California have long ago solidified into granite. Those ancient volcanoes, now eroded down to their roots, are surely dead.

The oldest volcanic foundation rocks in our national parks occur in the Midwest, the youngest in Hawaii. Isle Royale National Park and Keweenaw National Historic Park in Michigan are built on basaltic lava bedrock so old–1,200 million years—that their source volcanoes are long dead and gone. In contrast, the basaltic lava currently erupting from Kilauea Volcano is the newest rock on Earth.

The time a volcano sleeps between eruptions also varies greatly. The repose time of Kilauea Volcano in Hawaii during the past 200 years has averaged about a year. Neighboring Mauna Loa Volcano sleeps on average about four years between eruptions, but overslept for 26 years between eruptions from 1950 to 1976. Mount Rainier in Washington may doze for centuries or millennia between eruptions.

The life spans of volcanoes also vary greatly. A cinder cone like Capulin Volcano in New Mexico may form during a brief eruption that lasts only a few years. In contrast, the caldera in Yellowstone

▲ *Half Dome in Yosemite National Park, California, is an eroded remnant of an ancient magma chamber that once–100 million years ago–fed a chain of erupting volcanoes. The volcanoes have eroded away along with about five miles of rock that once covered the granites of Yosemite.*

J.D. Griggs, USGS

▲ Lava fountains from the early phase of the Pu'u O'o eruption of Kilauea Volcano in Hawaii sprayed as high as 1,500 feet. The helicopter in the upper left is so dwarfed by the incandescent fountain that it looks like a mosquito. Volcanic cinders formed by the fall-back of cooled lava fragments helped build the pu'u ("hill," in Hawaiian) at the base of the fountain.

National Park has disgorged three giant eruptions during the past two million years. Even so, two million years is only a tiny fraction of the 4.6 billion years since the Earth was born. Try this thought experiment: if all geologic time is reduced to a human life span of 70 years, by the same ratio, two million years reduces to just 11 days.

Human life span is so short compared to geologic time that we perceive the Earth as a fairly peaceful place. This snapshot of the world is misleading. Over just small fractions of geologic time, and sometimes, as at Mount St. Helens, in just a few minutes the Earth can change dramatically and violently.

Fortunately, one of the laws of Nature that helps maintain the Earth's tranquility is that extreme events, like the huge eruption at Yellowstone 630,000 years ago, are rare compared to smaller events. The bigger they are, the less often they happen. Volcanic eruptions,

Another way to get an increase in the silica content of magma is by melting and mixing crustal rocks into a rising body of basaltic magma. The temperature of basaltic magma at 2,200°F. is high enough to melt crustal rocks like granite, given the presence of water and sufficient time of contact between the basaltic magma and the crustal rocks.

Note that both these processes (partial crystallization or crustal contamination) that can generate andesite, dacite and rhyolite, involve basaltic magma in some fundamental way. That is the reason it is often called the mother rock. In the Azores, volcanic islands in the Atlantic Ocean, the farmers have a saying which translates into "the rocks are the mother of the soil." Basaltic magma must then be the grandmother.

▲ Shiny pahoehoe lava and dull, rough a'a lava have the same chemical composition. In general, pahoehoe flows are hotter and more fluid. If a pahoehoe flow partly cools and then moves more rapidly down a steep slope, its surface begins to break up into rough pieces and its texture converts into an a'a flow.

▲ *Lassen Peak seen from Lake Helen. This 10,457-foot-high stratovolcano is capped by a massive lava dome that grew about 27,000 years ago. Its latest activity, a complex explosive eruption that involved a summit lava flow, mudflows and a pyroclastic flow, occurred from 1914 to 1917.*

The illustration on page 35 identifies the prominent types of volcanoes. Most common are the stratovolcanoes—Mount Rainier in Washington State is a good example. A stratovolcano is conical, has steep sides, and often, like Mount Fuji in Japan, curves gracefully upwards with increasing steepness toward its summit. Its shape and beauty are what come to mind when most people think of the word "volcano." The name stratovolcano comes from the word strata, meaning layers. This type of volcano is composed of layers of both lava flows and explosive pyroclastic deposits. The name "composite volcano" is synonymous with stratovolcano.

Mudflows of volcanic debris from floods and landslides often form an apron of less-steep deposits around the base of a stratovolcano. These additional strata help to form the classic volcanic landscape—a gigantic conical mountain. The individual rocks and particles that build most stratovolcanoes range from basalt to rhyolite, but are mainly andesite.

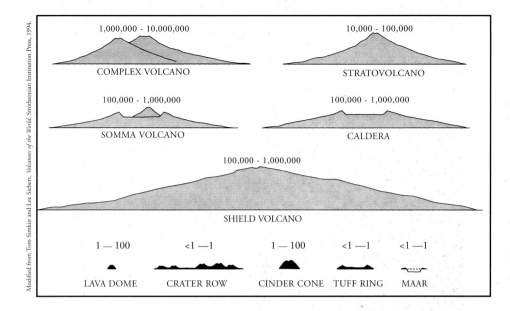

1,000,000 - 10,000,000

COMPLEX VOLCANO

10,000 - 100,000

STRATOVOLCANO

100,000 - 1,000,000

SOMMA VOLCANO

100,000 - 1,000,000

CALDERA

100,000 - 1,000,000

SHIELD VOLCANO

| 1 — 100 | <1 —1 | 1 — 100 | <1 —1 | <1 —1 |
| LAVA DOME | CRATER ROW | CINDER CONE | TUFF RING | MAAR |

A stratovolcano often undergoes some major modifications to its classic shape. Its summit may collapse into a large basin called a caldera, and the caldera basin sometimes fills with a beautiful circular lake, like Crater Lake in Oregon. Calderas on stratovolcanoes are generally caused by enormous explosive eruptions of dacite or rhyolite that drain the magma chamber beneath the volcano. This evisceration of the volcano is accompanied or quickly followed by collapse of the summit into the void below. The sudden disappearance of the entire summit of a huge volcano is sometimes reported as the volcano "blowing its top." It would be more accurate but more complex to say the volcano blew its heart out and its top fell in.

Sometimes a younger volcanic cone grows inside a caldera to form what is called a somma volcano. Mount Vesuvius in Italy is the classic example, and if Wizard Island in Crater Lake should grow to a height above the caldera rim, it would become a somma volcano. New vents at stratovolcanoes may build two or more summits in close proximity; this begets a new name—a complex volcano. Trident Volcano in Katmai National Park and Preserve, a cluster of five stratovolcanoes, is a good example of a complex volcano.

The term "shield volcano" comes from Iceland where a gently sloping volcanic mountain was first given this name. The term was inspired by the image of a giant warrior's shield lying face up on the ground. Mauna Loa Volcano in Hawaii Volcanoes National Park is the largest shield volcano in the world, and by volume the world's

▲ *Profiles of the relative sizes, shapes, and life spans of various types of volcanoes. Their approximate active life spans are indicated in years. Large shield volcanoes like Mauna Loa in Hawaii are much greater in volume but less imposing than stratovolcanoes like Mount Rainier.*

largest volcano of any type. Shield volcanoes are predominantly built of low viscosity, basaltic lava flows. Their gentle slopes reflect the low angle on which these fluid flows will continue to move downhill.

The summit of a shield volcano may also collapse to form a caldera. The calderas at the summits of Kilauea and Mauna Loa in Hawaii Volcanoes National Park owe their origin to much less violent and probably more prolonged eruptions than the great Crater Lake explosion. One theory is that voluminous flank eruptions of lava, perhaps deep below sea level, drained the magma chamber and caused step by step collapse of the summit as the flank eruption continued. The most recent collapse of Kilauea Caldera is thought to have occurred in 1790.

Smaller volcanic constructions include lava domes, crater rows, cinder cones, tuff rings, and maars. A lava dome is a steep mound of lava that is so viscous that it piles up over its erupting vent. The 1,000-foot-high lava dome that grew inside the horseshoe-shaped crater of Mount St. Helens during 1980 to 1986 is a good example. Lassen Peak is a large lava dome of prehistoric age. Radiometric dating techniques indicate that it extruded about 26,000 years ago. Most

▼ *Mount Rainier, a massive stratovolcano near Seattle, is 14,411 feet high. Its Native American name, Tahoma, simply means "The Mountain." Rainier's height about 5,500 years ago is estimated to have been about 16,000 feet before a major eruption and summit collapse. Its latest eruption occurred between AD 1820 and 1854.*

MOUNTAINS OF FIRE

lava domes are slow extrusions of dacite or rhyolite, viscous enough, but gas-poor enough, to form mounds over their vents. Some lava domes are blown apart by subsequent explosive eruptions.

A crater row is built by a fountaining lava eruption that takes place along a fissure. Eruption of low-viscosity lava in Hawaii Volcanoes National Park usually begins along a fissure in a spectacular display known as a curtain of fire. At wide places on the fissure, small cones of cinder and spatter mark the points where most of the eruptions of lava took place. In 1982, a fissure eruption in Kilauea Caldera built a crater row across part of the caldera floor. Crater rows are common on shield volcanoes that have rift zones—major fracture zones that rupture a volcano's sides. The ongoing Pu'u O'o eruption at Kilauea began in 1983 from a four-mile-long fissure zone that formed several small crater rows.

A cinder cone builds up around an erupting lava fountain—generally basaltic—where the lava fragments solidify before they fall back and pile up around the vent. The erupting lava is gas-rich enough to fountain, but low enough in viscosity not to explode. The loose cinders build a steep cone whose flanks slide if they become too steep. The resulting cone has a slope of about thirty

▲ *Wizard Island, a cinder cone, is a prominent feature in Crater Lake National Park. It grew following the caldera collapse and filling of the lake. The great explosive eruption and caldera collapse that formed the five- to six-mile-wide lake basin took place about 5700 BC. Beautiful blue Crater Lake is more than 1,900 feet deep, the deepest lake in the United States.*

degrees—the "angle of repose." If some of the fall-back lava fragments are still partly molten, the hill is called a spatter cone. Spatter cones may have sides even steeper than cinder cones because the spatter can weld into a strong mass. Sunset Crater Volcano in Arizona is a prehistoric cinder cone, and Pu'u O'o, the currently erupting vent on Hawaii's Kilauea Volcano is a combination cinder and spatter cone.

A tuff ring is a rim of explosion debris around a wide crater that was excavated by the blasts. Diamond Head, the famous volcanic landmark in Honolulu, is the high part of the rim of a classic tuff ring. If a wide explosion crater with a low rim of debris is excavated by volcanic eruptions in an area where the groundwater table is high, the crater fills with a circular lake known as a maar. Ukinrek Maars on the Alaska Peninsula erupted in 1977. They lie just to the west but outside of Katmai National Park and Preserve.

At times in the geologic past, but without any examples in recorded history, great floods of very fluid basaltic lava have poured from long fissures. The thick, extensive and nearly flat lava flows of the

Columbia River Plateau in Oregon and Washington that occurred 30 million years ago are a good example. These eruptions disgorge thousands of cubic miles of basalt. In contrast, the largest lava flow in recorded history occurred in Iceland in 1783. This fissure eruption created a crater row 15 miles long, and its three cubic miles of basalt flows covered nearly 200 square miles. The 1,200-million-year-old lava flows that form the bedrock of Isle Royale National Park and Keewanawan National Historic Park in Michigan are other ancient examples of flood basalts.

We are awed by the vast rhyolite explosions that formed the Yellowstone Caldera, and the enormous basalt flows of Michigan's Upper Peninsula. We are grateful they occurred in geologic history, not human history. But there is an old saying in geology, "What did happen, can happen."

Much is known about volcanic rocks and landscapes, but there is still much more to be learned about them and about how volcanoes work. The national parks are beautiful and wonderful places to study these majestic and mysterious mountains.

▼ *Prehistoric cinder cones near the summit of Mauna Kea, a higher but less massive shield volcano than Mauna Loa on the Island of Hawaii. Outside of the boundaries of Hawaii Volcanoes National Park, the summit area of 13,796-foot-high Mauna Kea is dotted with some of the world's best and most modern telescopes.*

VOLCANIC FEATURES

HOT SPRINGS AND GEYSERS

Features called geysers, fumaroles, boiling springs, mofettes, mud pots, and solfataras; places named Devil's Kitchen, Colter's Hell, and Sulphur Works—what playgrounds for the demons of the underworld. These vents of steam, hot water, sulfur gases and carbon dioxide are close relatives of volcanoes. Geysers are intermittent fountains of steam and hot water. Mud pots are bubbling pits of hot, thick, muddy water; fumaroles are gas vents, mostly of steam, but sometimes called mofettes if the gas is rich in carbon dioxide, or solfataras if sulfur gases are abundant. Lumped together they are called thermal features because in most cases the springs or gas vents are warm to hot, often scalding.

Almost all the hot water in thermal features is groundwater that has been heated by deep circulation into the roots of live or sleeping volcanoes. As the water is heated, perhaps at a depth of several thousand feet, it becomes less dense and rises back toward the surface. The sulfur gases—the rotten-egg smell of hydrogen sulfide, or the choking, acrid smell of sulfur dioxide—and carbon dioxide, which is odorless but suffocating in high concentrations, are more likely of direct volcanic origin. As the roots of volcanoes cool, these magmatic gases seep upward toward the surface. Some of the escaping gases on reaching shallow depths mix with oxygen-rich thermal waters to form a witch's brew of acid. They are weak acids from a chemist's view, but strong enough to dissolve some minerals and slowly digest hard rocks into soft clay.

Yellowstone National Park has the best and most extensive assemblage of thermal features in the world. Iceland and New Zealand also have wonderful geysers and hot springs, but we have seen all three places and declare Yellowstone the winner. The word "geyser" comes from Iceland, used long before trapper John Colter ever set foot in Yellowstone. *Geysir,* a word meaning "to gush," was the name given by Icelanders to its greatest spouting fountain of steam and hot water more than 700 years ago.

To understand geysers, and also geothermal power, it is important to know that the boiling point of water changes with pressure. Everyone who lives at high altitudes realizes that water boils there at

▶ *Opposite: The steaming vent of Riverside Geyser sits just beside the much cooler water in the Firehole River in Yellowstone National Park. A geyser is an intermittent fountain of hot water and steam. The word originally comes from Iceland, where geysers were first named and described.*

▲ Yellowstone's Old Faithful Geyser puts on a steamy show in winter. This famous geyser sprays up to 12,000 gallons of boiling water to heights of 100 to 150 feet about every 40 to 80 minutes. Each eruption lasts a few minutes and releases about one megawatt of power. Old Faithful's eruptions have been closely observed for more than 100 years, and have probably been fountaining for thousands of years.

less than 212°F. It takes longer to cook boiled potatoes in Denver than in New York because in Denver the boiling temperature of water is only 202°. It works the opposite way if you increase pressure by going underground. One hundred feet below the ground-water table, the boiling point of water is 287°F.; 1,000 feet down it's 445°. It is this characteristic of water that provides the power of geysers.

Imagine a 100-foot-deep pipe buried in the ground and filled with hot water near its boiling temperature. At the top of the pipe, let's say the water temperature is 211°, just below its boiling point. At the bottom of the pipe, the water temperature is 287°, just at its boiling point at that higher pressure. If boiling begins somewhere down in the pipe it forms a bubble of expanding steam that pushes some of the water out the top of the pipe. That overflow lowers the pressure at all depths in the pipe below the surface, and a runaway reaction begins to happen. More and more water begins to boil, and fountains out of the top of the pipe as a mixture of steam and boiling water.

MOUNTAINS OF FIRE

This lowers the pressure even more in the lower parts of the pipe, and even more water flashes to steam. This run-away reaction continues until all the hot water and steam have been boiled out of the pipe.

The conduits that supply real geysers are much more complex than a simple pipe, but the principle is the same. In nature, after the conduit boils itself empty in a spectacular geyser eruption, groundwater slowly refills the conduit. Volcanic heating resumes, and the process returns to a state where the run-away reaction is ready to go again. Overflow of hot water from the surface vent of a geyser is often a clue that it may be about to erupt.

Geysers are rare; there are fewer than 1,000 in the world. About 500 of them are in Yellowstone National Park, some 200 in Kamchatka, about 40 in New Zealand, and 16 in Iceland. Another 50 are scattered in many other volcanic areas. Thus Yellowstone has more than half of all the world's geysers. A geyser is rare because the combination of factors that makes it work is an unlikely coincidence: a high groundwater table with springs and pools at the surface; near-boiling temperatures a few feet below the ground surface; and a combination of underground fractures and chambers that form a reservoir and conduit below the geyser vent.

▼ *Mineralized hot water flowing down hillsides at Mammoth Hot Springs, in northern Yellowstone National Park, have formed spectacular terraces of travertine deposits. Trails wind through the extensive area of dormant and still-flowing terraces with names like Minerva, Cleopatra, Mound, Opal, Jupiter and Hymen.*

Don Pitcher

Some geysers erupt on a fairly regular schedule. Old Faithful in Yellowstone spouts some 100,000 pounds of boiling water and steam on roughly an hourly timetable. The fountain reaches a height of about 125 feet, and lasts for a few minutes. Recorded intervals between eruptions range from 30 to 120 minutes, with an average of 80 minutes. If Old Faithful's eruption lasts only a minute or two, the next interval will be shorter than average, while a four-minute eruption will be followed by a longer quiet interval.

Giant Geyser, another of Yellowstone's more famous, can fountain to nearly 300 feet, but its eruption intervals have varied from days to years. Major changes to many geysers happened following a magnitude 7.5 earthquake that rattled Yellowstone in 1959. Within hours and during the next few days, hundreds of geysers erupted, including some new ones. Even Old Faithful changed its habits; its average interval between eruptions increased a few minutes compared to the pre-1959 average. The shaking apparently induced the unusual burst of activity of many geysers just

▲ Bumpass Hell, a geothermal area in Lassen Volcanic National Park. Old-timer Kendall Bumpass discovered this place years ago. Unfortunately he lost a leg from the scalding burns he received from breaking through the crust surrounding a boiling mud pot.

following the quake, and the longer-term changes may be related to new fractures created in the conduits and interconnections between closely-spaced geysers and hot springs.

If a hot spring fountains continuously it is usually called a boiling spring rather than a geyser, and if the water and clay in a boiling hot spring mix into thick mud, the name becomes mud pot. The large bubbles that slowly form beneath the surface of a mud pot look momentarily like sunny-side-up fried eggs, except they are an unappetizing gray.

The clay in mud pots and the dangerous scalding mud that often surrounds hot spring areas comes from the breakdown of volcanic rocks by the hot water percolating through them. This type of rock disintegration is common in volcanic areas; geologists call it "hydrothermal alteration." The deep canyon of the Yellowstone River has cut down into a major zone of hydrothermal alteration where the rocks have rotted to earthy yellows and browns.

Hot water circulating through bedrock dissolves silica; the hotter the water, the more silica it dissolves. When the water cools, for example in a geyser eruption, dissolved silica is precipitated as a light gray material called siliceous sinter. The castles and grottos of rock built up around the vents of geysers are composed of this sinter. Some geysers just build a low dome or platform of sinter around their vents. If the waters feeding hot springs have circulated through limestone underground, they dissolve calcium carbonate

▼ *Mud pot in Bumpass Hell, Lassen Volcanic National Park. Mud pots are better seen in video. A bubble a few inches across slowly grows until it looks like the yolk of a frying egg, sunny side up— but gray instead of yellow and white. The bubble bursts and the process repeats.*

Rings of colored bacteria surround the nearly 400-foot-wide Grand Prismatic Spring in Yellowstone National Park. As the scalding hot water cools by flowing across the sides of the pool, different types (and colors) of bacteria grow in the water temperature most suited to their growth.

that on cooling precipitates deposits called travertine. The steaming terraces at Mammoth Hot Springs in Yellowstone are walled in by beautiful ledges of colored travertine.

Some of the colors in siliceous sinter and travertine are from iron oxides and other minerals, but most of the color in hot springs and steaming terraces is from thermophile (heat-loving) microorganisms. One of the more common of these microscopic creatures that thrive in hot water is cyanobacteria, which grow in huge colonies called bacterial mats. These mats form colorful scums and slimes on the sides of hot springs and bottoms of run-off streams. Various colors of cyanobacteria prefer particular water chemistry and temperature, thus providing a rough thermometer of hot springs: yellow about 160°F.; orange about 145°; brown about 130°; and green about 120° or lower. In more acid hot springs green algae become the dominant microorganism, but they do not exhibit the rings or bands of colors like the cyanobacteria.

Biologists have become increasingly interested in thermophile microorganisms for several reasons. They want to discover how life survives at high temperatures, and they want to know more about potentially useful organic chemicals that some of these organisms synthesize. It is also apparent that some species of these creatures are closer to the base of the "tree of life" than any other. If so, places like Yellowstone and hot springs on the deep ocean floor may help to unlock the secret of the origin of life.

Studies of these heat-loving microorganisms and their genes have already led to a new addition to the kingdoms of life. This new branch, called Archaea, is low on the evolutionary tree, near or just above bacteria. Craig Venter, leader of the team of scientists who mapped the 1,738 genes in Archaea from submarine hot-spring vents along a mid-ocean rift zone, remarked that "two thirds of its genes don't look like anything we've ever seen in biology before." Some Archaea of the deep-sea hot springs live in total darkness on a diet of carbon dioxide, hydrogen, nitrogen and heat, and produce methane.

Several varieties of these puzzling one-celled Archaea are found in the hot springs of Yellowstone. Their organic chemistry and metabolisms are the subject of intensive current research. Among the startling discoveries are the very high temperatures to which some of these heat-loving cells can survive. A few of the present record-holders can be cultured in water under pressure at temperatures exceeding 212ºF., the boiling point of water at sea level.

▼ *Gem Pool in the Upper Geyser Basin of Yellowstone National Park. The mineral deposits on the rim of this hot spring are composed of silica, dissolved from rocks at depth by hot water, and precipitated back to solid form as the water cools.*

▲ *Hot springs keep Yellowstone's Sunset Lake constantly steaming on cool days. It is one of several hot pools in the Black Sand Basin, just northwest of Old Faithful. Overflow from the lake feeds colorful beds of algae.*

In places where the ground-water table is well below the land surface, as it is in most of the higher elevations of Hawaii Volcanoes National Park, hot springs and pools do not occur. Instead, fumaroles are the dominant thermal features. These volcanic gas vents emit steam, carbon dioxide, sulfur dioxide, and lesser amounts of hydrogen sulfide, hydrochloric acid, hydrogen, carbon monoxide, and hydrofluoric acid. Most of the gas is water vapor, and most of that comes from groundwater heated by volcanic rocks. Vents emitting both sulfur dioxide (SO_2) and hydrogen sulfide (H_2S) may deposit crystals of pure sulfur at the vent. The two sulfur gases react with one another, forming water and elemental sulfur.

During Mark Twain's visit to Hawaii more than a century ago, he wrote about his encounter with foul volcanic gases, "The smell of sulfur is strong, but not unpleasant to a sinner." The ongoing Pu'u O'o eruption in Hawaii puts out some 2,000 tons of sulfur dioxide a day, more than a major coal-fired power plant, and where the lava enters the ocean the resulting steam is laced with hydrochloric acid. This combination produces vog (volcanic smog) that quickly becomes diluted enough to lose its odor, but still thick enough to reduce visibility on the lee side of the Big Island.

Although volcanic gases may temporarily pollute the Earth's atmosphere, they have, over geologic time, helped to create our air and oceans. Most scientists studying the Earth's origin agree that volcanic gases are a significant source of water and carbon dioxide, but they also point out that comets striking the young Earth may have been the principal source of the atmosphere and oceans.

Stroll along the boardwalks past the boiling springs and mud pots of Bumpass Hell, but don't stray off the paths. You could lose a leg from scalding, as did Kendall Bumpass, its discoverer. Sniff the sulfur and think about the colorful microorganisms that may be living representatives of our oldest ancestors. In breathing the clear air of the pine forest on the trail back, and peering into the blue water of Lake Helen across the road, remember that volcanoes have helped create a heaven as well.

▼ *Sulfur crystals depositing around a fumarole in Kilauea Caldera, Hawaii Volcanoes National Park. The temperature of these sulfur-depositing fumaroles is generally hotter than the boiling point of water. As the gases cool down the steam cloud of condensing water droplets becomes visible.*

Part Two

VOLCANOES ALIVE

The only erupting volcano in our national parks and monuments at the time of this writing (2001) is Kilauea Volcano in Hawaii. The state of Hawaii is a chain of volcanic islands. Kilauea is located on the Island of Hawaii, more informally known as the Big Island to avoid the confusion of names between the state and its largest island.

All the other volcanoes in Part Two erupted one or more times during the 20th century. Mauna Loa, a close neighbor of Kilauea, last erupted in 1984. Its summit and part of its eastern flank are located in Hawaii Volcanoes National Park.

Mount St. Helens in Washington State erupted from 1980 to 1986, and Lassen Peak in California from 1914 to 1917. Other Cascade volcanoes are considered to be potentially active, but since they did not erupt during the 20th century they are described in Part Three, "Volcanoes Asleep."

Alaska can claim most of the volcanoes that produced lava or ash in the United States during the 20th century. Aniakchak Volcano, in a national monument of the same name, is a large caldera that last erupted in 1931. Katmai, Novarupta, and Trident Volcanoes are in Katmai National Park and Preserve. The great eruption of Novarupta and Katmai in 1912 was the world's largest of the century, and Trident's latest eruption was in 1974. Redoubt Volcano in Lake Clark National Park and Preserve had a significant eruption in 1990, and Wrangell Volcano in Wrangell-St. Elias National Park and Preserve erupted in the early 1900s.

Opposite: *Pu'u O'o vent, Kilauea Volcano, Hawaii. This vent began erupting in 1983, and at this writing (2001) is still pouring out molten lava.*
Below: *Valley of Ten Thousand Smokes, Katmai National Park, Alaska. When this photo was taken in the early 1960s, Trident Volcano was erupting in the background.*

National Park Service

HAWAII VOLCANOES NATIONAL PARK, HAWAII

▼ Lava entering the sea on the southeast coast of Kilauea Volcano. Great bubbles of steam created by molten lava contacting sea water often explode in combined bursts of incandescent lava and steam. The lava reaches the sea by flowing in lava tubes several miles long from the Pu'u O'o vent area.

If you want the chance to watch the incredible spectacle of a live volcano in action, a trip to Hawaii Volcanoes National Park is your best bet, for two reasons. First, Kilauea is probably the most active volcano in the world, and certainly in the United States. Its latest eruption started in 1983 and, except for short pauses, has continued for 18 years. At this writing (in the year 2001), it is still continuing. No guarantees, of course; it could stop tomorrow or keep erupting for many years. Still, it has already provided millions of visitors with an unforgettable experience.

Second, the nature of Hawaiian eruptions makes this a relatively safe place to watch one of Nature's grandest sound and light shows. Eruptions of Hawaii's hot-spot volcanoes are described as quiet, though "quiet" is not the first word that comes to mind when a fiery fountain of molten lava shoots 1,500 feet into the air with the roar of a jet engine. They are considered quiet only in contrast to the devastating and dangerous explosive eruptions that are common at stratovolcanoes along subduction zones. Hawaii's volcanoes erupt effusively instead of explosively, meaning with an outpouring of lava flows that build a "shield" of many layers and can travel for miles.

USGS

Lava flows can be devastating to property, but are rarely life threatening. The two types of eruptions are different mostly because of the gas content and viscosity of the lava, as explained in Part One.

But even if the volcanoes are at rest when you are in Hawaii, the dramatic volcanic scenery will give you an eerie sense of their immense power, and you will see some of the newest rocks on Earth.

Hawaii Volcanoes National Park is large for an island park—340 square miles, with more being added as flows from Kilauea pour into the sea. The park extends from sea level to more than 13,000 feet at the summit of Mauna Loa, the park's other active volcano, which last erupted in 1984. Moisture-laden trade winds move up the windward slopes, cooling and dropping immense amounts of rain; on the lee side they descend, warm and dry out. Within a few miles you can go from humid tropics to the hot Kau Desert, and from cool, misty forests to open areas of snow-covered, rocky terrain above timberline.

The accessibility of the volcanoes in Hawaii Volcanoes National Park, their frequent eruptions, and the protection of the natural scene afforded by national park status makes this a nearly ideal place for volcanologists to study how volcanoes work.

▲ *The snow-covered summit of Mauna Loa, a 13,677-foot-high shield volcano, is indented by a 3- by 1.5-mile-wide caldera, as well as by lesser craters. Mauna Kea Volcano is visible in the background, to the north. Mauna Loa's caldera is thought to have formed by removal of magma from a chamber about three miles beneath its summit, perhaps by a major prehistoric eruption far down one of its rift zones.*

The Hawaiian Volcano Observatory has operated here on the edge of Kilauea Crater since 1912, and is one of the leading volcano research facilities in the world. Here scientists monitor the vital signs of Kilauea and Mauna Loa using seismographs, tiltmeters and other sophisticated electronic instruments. Seismometers record more than 100,000 tiny earthquakes every year, most too slight to be felt by human senses. When seismometers detect a nearly-continuous vibration called harmonic tremor, it is a sign that magma is moving in fractures underground and an eruption may be imminent. A tiltmeter works on the same principle as an incredibly sensitive carpenter's level, able to measure changes of one part in 10 million. In the months or years before an eruption the volcano inflates as magma pushes upward, so the tiltmeter shows the ground at the summit tilting away from the caldera. When an eruption takes place or when magma moves underground into one of the rift zones, the summit deflates and the tiltmeter registers tilting inward toward the caldera.

Volcanologists also measure the composition, volume and temperature of gases emitted from the volcano. They study the Earth's electrical and magnetic fields near the summits and rift zones. They use satellite surveying methods to measure how Kilauea's south flank is inching toward the sea. The laboratories at the Hawaiian Volcano Observatory are not open to the public, but the adjacent Jaggar Museum, named for the founder of the observatory, has fine exhibits about the volcanoes and how scientists study them.

Other important studies at Hawaii Volcanoes National Park are of the way plants and animals recover and recolonize an area that has been devastated by lava flows. This gives a partial clue to the way life could have arrived and taken hold on this isolated chain of islands, 2,500 miles from the nearest continental neighbor. The adaptation and evolution by the few seeds, birds and insects that accidentally arrived here have been so remarkable that it is often said that if Darwin had seen Hawaii before the Galapagos he would never have left. Today's Hawaiian mood and lifestyle may be leisurely and laid back compared to other parts of the world, but Hawaii's geology—and to a large part its evolutionary processes—run at high speeds.

Of the two volcanoes in Hawaii Volcanoes National Park, Mauna Loa is much the larger, but Kilauea, the youngest volcano on the Island of Hawaii, is the easiest to see up close. A road circles the caldera, which formed in a huge eruption in 1790. Inside the caldera is a pit crater called Halemaumau, the legendary home of Pele,

◄ Opposite: An arching lava fountain about 30 feet high pours from an early vent of the Pu'u O'o eruption. You can probably guess that this photo (by J.D. Griggs with the U.S. Geological Survey) was taken with a telephoto lens. Orange-hot lava, even hotter than red-hot lava, has a temperature of about 2,100° Fahrenheit. If you were standing within 30 to 40 feet of this vent, the radiant heat would singe your hair.

▲ **Above:** *A slow-moving a'a lava flow typically builds in height as it swells from within, and then surges rapidly forward. In this case geologists who had been taking measurements had to outrun its fast advance.*

▼ **Below:** *A rare dome fountain of lava, about 20 feet across, wells from an erupting vent on Kilauea Volcano.*

Goddess of Hawaiian Volcanoes. Off and on in Kilauea's history, Halemaumau has been filled with a lake of red, molten lava. Kilauea's eruptions take place here at the summit or along two zones of weakness on its flanks, the East and South West Rift Zones.

Kilauea's latest flank eruption, the longest running in Hawaii's recorded history, has taken place from several vents on the East Rift Zone. It began in January, 1983, with intermittent fountaining called a "curtain of fire," along a line of fissures nine miles east of the summit. By June the fissures had localized to a single vent that geologists named Pu'u O'o—Hill of the *O'o,* an extinct Hawaiian bird.

Over the next three years Pu'u O'o erupted more than 40 times, with spectacular fountains as high as 1,500 feet. Each episode lasted about a day, alternating with quiet periods of about 25 days. Fallback from the fountains built up a cone around the vent that grew to a height of 843 feet. The flows from Pu'u O'o were mostly a'a, slow-moving flows with a rubble of solidified, broken lava

VOLCANOES ALIVE

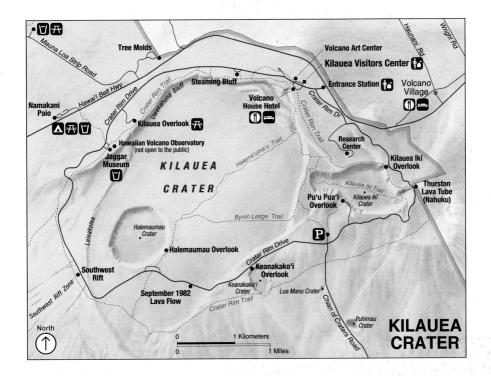

KILAUEA
CRATER

North
↑

0 ——— 1 Kilometers
0 ——— 1 Miles

blocks riding on top. None of those flows reached the ocean or the highway, but they crashed through native forest and into a rural subdivision called Royal Gardens, destroying many homes and cutting access roads.

Then in July 1986 the activity shifted, this time to a vent downrift that geologists named Kupaianaha, meaning mysterious. The character of the eruption changed too; instead of Pu'u O'o's geyserlike, intermittent fountains of lava, Kupaianaha continuously poured out flows of pahoehoe. The two types of flows—pahoehoe and a'a—are so characteristic of Hawaiian volcanoes that the Hawaiian names are used all over the world for similar flows.

While an a'a flow has a chunky, angular, jagged surface, a pahoehoe flow is smooth and billowy, sometimes with a ropy look to its shiny skin. Oddly enough, the chemical composition of both is the same; the difference seems to be that an a'a flow is cooler and has lost some of its gas content, so internal crystals increase and the flow starts to break up.

Fast-moving pahoehoe flows form channels, and gradually crust over. This allows the lava to course through a "lava tube" or tunnel without much heat loss, so it can travel a great distance.

▲ An 11-mile long road known as "Crater Rim Drive" circles the summit caldera of Kilauea Volcano. Stops and views along the way include Kilauea Iki Crater, Thurston Lava Tube (Nahuku), Devastation Trail, Keanakako'i Crater, Halemaumau Crater (the legendary home of the goddess Pele), cracks of the Southwest Rift Zone and the Jaggar Museum.

This is what happened at Kupaianaha. As lava tubes formed, tube-fed pahoehoe relentlessly advanced toward the coast. After cutting the coast road in November 1986, flows poured into the ocean. Over the next few years the lava changed course several times, with surface flows overrunning a park visitor center and a *heiau*, ancient Hawaiian temple, and moving through the community of Kalapana, where it destroyed more than 100 homes.

By 1992 there were signs that Pele wanted to go back to Pu'u O'o. Kupaianaha was waning and soon died; a few days later pahoehoe flows started from vents on the flanks of the Pu'u O'o cone. In the years since, a large part of the Pu'u O'o cone has collapsed, while several pauses have caused speculation that the long-lived eruption might be over. And yet, it keeps coming back to life. As of now (2001) there is no way to guess when it might end. There is evidence that one prehistoric flank eruption lasted for about 70 years, but every eruption has its own story.

▲ **Above:** Ohelo berries, sacred to Pele, are sometimes thrown as offerings into Halemaumau Crater.

▼ **Below:** During the 1984 eruption of Mauna Loa Volcano, lava flows threatened the city of Hilo, seen in the foreground above the trees. The night view was especially ominous, but fortunately the eruption stopped before the flows reached the outskirts of town.

Mauna Loa last erupted in March 1984, after a nine-year nap. Earthquakes and inflation had been accelerating during 1983, so scientists had a general idea that an eruption was coming, although Mauna Loa gave no hints of just when it would happen. Lava fountains first broke the surface in a curtain of fire at Mauna Loa's summit, lighting the night sky with a fiery glow. Over the next day the vents migrated northeast, down the mountain to the 9,400-foot level. Flows were fast-moving and voluminous, and were heading for the city of Hilo.

Hard levees of cooling lava built up on the edges of the flow, confining it to a narrow channel. The speed slowed somewhat, but the view from Hilo—especially at night, when the glowing flows and fume clouds looked terrifying—was more and more ominous.

But then Hilo was granted a reprieve that seemed almost like a miracle. An upslope levee along the main lava channel broke, diverting most of the lava into a parallel flow and slowing its advance. Over the next week more levee breaks and diversions took place even farther upslope, letting the lava spread out instead of advancing relentlessly downhill. Lava production from the vent gradually slowed, and on April 15 the eruption was over. Hilo was out of danger this time, but any city downslope from an active volcano knows it can't be too complacent.

VOLCANOES ALIVE

Both the Mauna Loa eruption and the current Kilauea activity have been a bonanza for volcanologists trying to understand the mysterious ways of these restless mountains. Almost every eruption reveals the answer to some question, but the added knowledge often raises new questions. One long-standing question that was at least partly answered in this case concerned how closely related the underground systems of these two volcanoes are. Kilauea's Pu'u O'o was in its intermittent phase, fountaining about once a month, when the Mauna Loa eruption started. Speculation ran high as to whether the voluminous flows from Mauna Loa would steal Kilauea's lava supply, but on March 30, 1984, Kilauea's next fountaining episode arrived right on schedule. This seems to prove that while Mauna Loa and Kilauea are fed by the same deep hot spot, each has its own conduit and a separate magma chamber. Whatever the scientific explanation, for one night Big Islanders were treated to the grand sight of their two volcanoes erupting at the same time—only the second time that has happened in a century.

▲ *Above:* A lava lake in Kilauea Iki Crater lapped up on lush rainforest vegetation, leaving this stark contrast in textures.

▼ *Below:* Where a tiny crease in a recently cooled pahoehoe lava flow can hold a bit of water, ferns such as this one are among the first plants to colonize.

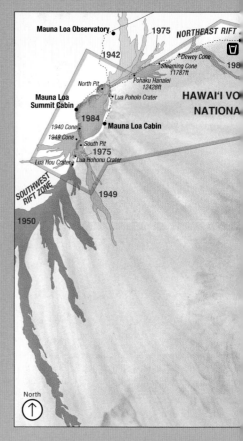

Map labels: Mauna Loa Observatory · 1975 · NORTHEAST RIFT · 1942 · Dewey Cone · Steaming Cone 11787ft · 198 · North Pit · Pohaku Hanalei 12428ft · HAWAI'I VO · NATIONA · Mauna Loa Summit Cabin · Lua Poholo Crater · 1984 · Mauna Loa Cabin · 1940 Cone · 1949 Cone · South Pit · 1975 · Lua Hou Crater · Lua Hohonu Crater · SOUTHWEST RIFT ZONE · 1949 · 1950

North ↑

▸ GETTING THERE

Hawaii Volcanoes National Park is on the southeast side of the Big Island of Hawaii. Fly to Hilo or Kona. From Hilo drive 30 miles southwest on State Highway 11 to the Park. From Kona Airport, drive 7 miles south on State Highway 19 to Kailua-Kona, then 110 miles on State Highway 11 counter-clockwise around the island to the park.

J.D. Griggs, USGS

A plume of steam rises where molten lava enters the sea on the southeast coastline of Kilauea Volcano, on the Big Island of Hawaii.

▸ ESSENTIALS

The park is open and entrance fees are collected year round. Roads are open day and night. Food and lodging are available at Volcano House (808-967-7321) in the park, and in the village of Volcano, just north of the park. Campgrounds are available, but no gasoline.

▸ CLIMATE

Warm year round except at high elevations on Mauna Loa Volcano. Rainy to dry with quick changes.

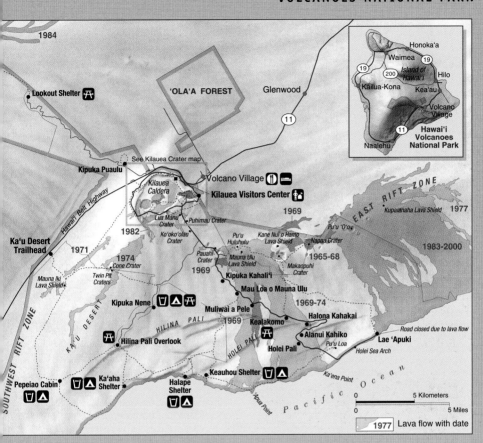

HAWAII
VOLCANOES NATIONAL PARK

1984

Lookout Shelter

'OLA'A FOREST

Glenwood

11

Honoka'a
Waimea
19
Island of
Hawai'i
Kailua-Kona
Kea'au
Hilo
Volcano
Village
11
Hawai'i
Volcanoes
National Park
Naalehu

Kipuka Puaulu

See Kilauea Crater map

Kilauea
Caldera

Volcano Village

Kilauea Visitors Center

EAST RIFT ZONE

1969

Kupaianaha Lava Shield

1977

Hawaii Belt Highway

Lua Manu
Crater
Puhimau Crater

1982

Ko'oko'olau
Crater

Pu'u 'O'o

Pu'u
Huluhulu

Kane Nui o Hamo
Lava Shield

Napau Crater

1983-2000

Ka'u Desert
Trailhead

1971

Pauahi
Crater

Mauna Ulu
Lava Shield

1965-68

Makaopuhi
Crater

1974

Cone Crater

1969

Kipuka Kahali'i

Mauna Iki
Lava Shield

Twin Pit
Craters

Mau Loa o Mauna Ulu

1969-74

Kipuka Nene

Muliwai a Pele

Halona Kahakai

SOUTHWEST RIFT ZONE

KA'U DESERT

HILINA PALI

1969

Kealakomo

Road closed due to lava flow

Hilina Pali Overlook

HOLEI PALI

Alanui Kahiko

Pu'u Loa

Lae 'Apuki

Holei Pali

Holei Sea Arch

Pepeiao Cabin

Ka'aha
Shelter

Keauhou Shelter

Ka'ena Point

Halape
Shelter

Aqua Point

Pacific Ocean

0   5 Kilometers
0   5 Miles

1977 Lava flow with date

▶ INFORMATION

Hawaii Volcanoes National Park
Post Office Box 52
Hawaii National Park,
Hawaii, 96718
Telephone: 808-985-6000
Website: www.nps.gov/havo

▶ VOLCANO FACTS

Name – Kilauea
Volcano type – shield volcano with caldera
Rock type – basalt
Height – 4,093 feet
Latest eruption – AD 2001

Name – Mauna Loa Volcano
Volcano type – shield volcano with caldera
Rock type – basalt
Height – 13,667 feet
Latest eruption – AD 1984

MOUNT ST. HELENS
NATIONAL VOLCANIC MONUMENT, WASHINGTON

▶ **Opposite:** *The Meta Lake area, eight miles north-east of the summit of Mount St. Helens, was devastated by the May 18, 1980, erup-tion. The young alpine fir trees growing in this photo, taken in 1992, were small enough to be protected by snow cover during the blast.*

▼ **Below:** *The beautifully symmetrical profile of 9,677-foot-high Mount St. Helens, as it appeared before the 1980 eruption, was some-times likened to Japan's famous Mount Fuji.*

At Mount St. Helens National Volcanic Monument you can see dramatic evidence of Nature's two faces—the tremendous destruc-tive power of natural forces, and the tenacious resilience of life. On May 18, 1980, a huge eruption—only the second of the 20th cen-tury in the contiguous United States—reduced Mount St. Helens from a graceful cone 9,677 feet high to a blasted stump of only 8,365 feet. The hot, dense explosion cloud blew trees down like toothpicks and killed almost everything in its path.

The eruption was not unexpected. Scientists had been carefully monitoring the volcano's vital signs since it first stirred to life two months earlier. The surprise was the size and ferocity of the eruption. In the years since then, other scientists from all over the world have come to Mount St. Helens to study how life—in its many forms—returns to a landscape that has been so devastatingly altered. Their surprises have been many, including the speed of recovery in an area some feared would be barren for many years, and the succession of regrowth which seems to contradict classical ecological theory.

But first the story of the eruption itself. After slumbering for 123 years, Mount St. Helens shook itself awake with a swarm of earthquakes that began on March 20, 1980. More and more small quakes were felt over the next week; then a more serious sign appeared. Small ash eruptions began at the summit, over the next few weeks excavating a small crater and covering the snow-capped mountain with a shroud of black ash. The steam explosions were from heated ground-water, an ominous sign that magma was rising inside the volcano.

▲ *Parked at a lumbering site 10 miles northwest of the blast on May 18, 1980, this bulldozer was wrecked like a toy. If the eruption had not occurred on a Sunday, many lumber workers would have been killed.*

As the intermittent earthquakes continued, scientists who were taking measurements of the mountain saw a huge bulge starting to grow high on the north flank of Mount St. Helens. It was expanding at the alarming rate of three to six feet a day, a change visible to the naked eye.

By the middle of May the bulge had grown to more than a mile and a half in diameter and had expanded more than 400 feet to the north. Earthquakes centered below the bulge were another sign that magma was moving upward and inflating the mountain. An avalanche from the north side seemed a likely scenario. Everyone was alert and waiting, but no one was really prepared for the chaos that followed.

On Sunday, May 18—a calm, sunny morning—an incredible sequence of events began. At 8:32 a.m. a magnitude 5.1 earthquake suddenly struck, centered below the bulging north slope. That oversteepened mountainside broke loose and crashed down in the largest avalanche in recorded history, tearing through Spirit Lake at an estimated 200 miles per hour. One part of the landslide climbed over a 1,200-foot-high ridge six miles to the north, while the main part raced down the North Fork of the Toutle River for 17 miles, filling the valley with debris that in some places was 600 feet thick.

As the avalanche slid away, a huge lateral blast—a cloud of superheated gas, steam, hot ash and rock fragments, called by some a "stone wind"—shot out of the mountain. Moving at speeds estimated to be as high as 625 miles per hour, the blast overtook the avalanche and swept across the landscape to the north, east and west, leveling 230 square miles of old-growth forest. Close to the crater, trees six feet in diameter were shredded and blown away. Farther away, trees were blown down or snapped off, their scoured trunks pointing downwind. Up to this point only five minutes had passed since the earthquake that triggered the landslide.

▼ *A geologist lands by helicopter on a pumice deposit from the July 22, 1980, pyroclastic flow at the north base of Mount St. Helens. Pumice is so filled with gas bubble holes that a person can lift a piece the size of a large boulder.*

USGS

The top of the magma column was now uncovered, letting a hot ash cloud jet upward 17 miles into the sky. The lower, dense parts of the ash cloud formed pyroclastic flows of hot rock fragments fluidized by expanding gas. Those flows surged out of the mountain's shattered crater, racing toward Spirit Lake and covering part of the avalanche deposits.

The last event in this catastrophic sequence was the forming of mudflows—floods of water from melting ice, the groundwater-soaked avalanche and the slosh from Spirit Lake, mixed with rocks, ash and debris—poured down the streams and rivers around Mount St. Helens. The worst mudflow was on the North Fork of the Toutle River. Houses and bridges were swept away by the hot, dense mud. The flow reached all the way to the Columbia River, clogging its shipping channel for months.

Fifty-seven people died in the eruption, including a young USGS geologist named David Johnston who had been monitoring the volcano's vital signs from a site that, in retrospect, was much too close. On that spot today the Johnston Ridge Visitor Center frames the most dramatic view in the monument.

▼ *Before the devastating eruption of 1980, this bridge spanned the Toutle River, a great fishing stream that drains into the Cowlitz River, a major tributary of the Columbia River.*

USGS

Property damage totaled 1.5 billion dollars, and the toll on wildlife—large and small—was huge. An estimated 1,500 elk and 5,000 deer, not to mention countless small animals, birds and insects, were in the wrong place that day.

During the summer that followed the main eruption, it was evident that Mount St. Helens was still restless. A lava dome started to grow in the blasted crater, made up of lava so viscous that it piled up over the vent instead of flowing away. Three times between July and October a dome grew, only to be blown apart by an explosive eruption. These explosions were far smaller than the main eruption, but their ash clouds were high and impressive.

Between the last of that explosive series and 1986, a new dome grew in pulses, but without disruption, to its present height of about 1,000 feet. No one knows what the next act will be. The dome could remain stable for many years, or it could grow slowly and make a new summit for Mount St. Helens. It's also possible that it could blow itself apart and start the dome-building process all over again.

In the years since the great 1980 eruption, Mount St. Helens has proved to be an ideal place to study the complex interactions that allow ecosystems to respond to large-scale disturbances. It is often said that recovery depends on both survivors and colonizers, but here many other influences were at work, too. Our favorite John Muir quote, "When we try to pick out anything by itself, we find it hitched to everything else in the universe," is amply illustrated at Mount St. Helens.

▲ During the mudflow that followed the eruption, thousands of logs from a lumber storage area were swept like battering rams down the Toutle River, destroying the sturdy bridge that appears on the opposite page.

One important factor in the survival and recovery of life around the volcano was the time of year—mid-spring—that the eruption took place. Tiny rodents like pocket gophers and deer mice were safe in their burrows under the snow pack, and emerged later into a moonscape scene. But they brought out with them organic soil and fungi where windblown seeds could take root. The snowbanks also sheltered small trees and other plants, leaving islands of living foliage when the summer melt arrived.

Snow and ice had a profound effect on the lakes' survival too. The lakes and streams closest to the mountain were inundated with rocks, trees, debris, hot ash and dead animals, completely altering the water chemistry. The lakes at higher elevations were luckier; protected by a layer of ice and snow, a population of fish, frogs, salamanders and even some newts and muskrats were able to survive. Lakes like Spirit Lake were so damaged that scientists wondered if they could ever recover and support life again, but within five years the water chemistry—with the help of rain, melting snow, wind and waves—was almost back to pre-eruption levels.

Interactions between survivors and colonizers, both plant and animal life, have been so wonderfully complex that scientists from all over the world have conducted research projects here, some last-

▲ **Above:** The steaming lava dome inside the crater of Mount St. Helens, seen across Spirit Lake in 1982, grew to about 1,000 feet high in pulses of eruption between 1980 and 1986. Will there be future eruptions of Mount St. Helens? Yes. When? No one knows.

VOLCANOES ALIVE

ing for many years. Park Scientist Peter Frenzen says, "...the variety of 'experimental' settings created by the volcano have become an important laboratory for testing those ideas.... Animals, from the tiniest wood-boring insect to the largest elk, appear to be having a profound influence on the developing vegetation. Animals are selecting and colonizing areas on the basis of habitat characteristics and, in turn, helping to shape habitat structure and composition.... Plants representing all major stages of forest development appear to be establishing simultaneously. This contradicts classic ecological theory that describes the orderly establishment and successive replacement of one group of plants by another."

USGS

Early fears that it might take decades for plant and animal recovery to proceed have been largely unfounded. By 1983, 90 percent of plant species originally growing at Mount St. Helens could be found, though varying in number and dominant species by location. By 1985 the numbers of elk and deer were back to normal, and by 2000 there were three times more North American elk in the monument than before the 1980 eruption. The magnificent conifer forests around Mount St. Helens are also recovering in two very different ways. Inside the monument itself, 172 square miles were set aside as a living laboratory to study how Nature heals itself without

▲ **Above:** *Huge conifer trees were snapped off like matchsticks by the great blast of gas, rocks and volcanic ash from the eruption.*

▼ **Below:** *Near Ryan Lake a carpet of fireweed, the advance guard of nature's amazing recovery process, grows up against a wall of trees charred by the blast, but still standing.*

George Wuerthner

▲ **Above:** *Boulders and dried mud attest to the mud-flow that devastated the volcano's south side.*

▼ **Below:** *Bunchberry dog-wood grows from the volcanic ash a few years after the great eruption.*

▶ **Opposite:** *Topsoil and trees were scraped away by a mudflow in Lava Canyon, exposing bedrock lava.*

human intervention. Outside the monument on lands administered by the U.S. Forest Service and by private logging companies, downed trees were salvaged for lumber and millions of small trees replanted.

One of the questions most frequently asked of the rangers here is "Could Mount St. Helens erupt again?" The answer is "of course." The record that geologists can read in the deposits around the volcano shows that the long, slow cycle of destruction and renewal has happened many times in the past 40,000 years, with no indication that things are different now. But a huge eruption like the 1980 blast is very unlikely to take place without warning. The U.S. Geological Survey, the University of Washington, and the U.S. Forest Service carefully monitor Mount St. Helens and would close access to the mountain if they see signs of reawakening. No one can guess whether that might come in days, decades or centuries, but one geologist has remarked, "Mount St. Helens hasn't yet done all the dances she knows."

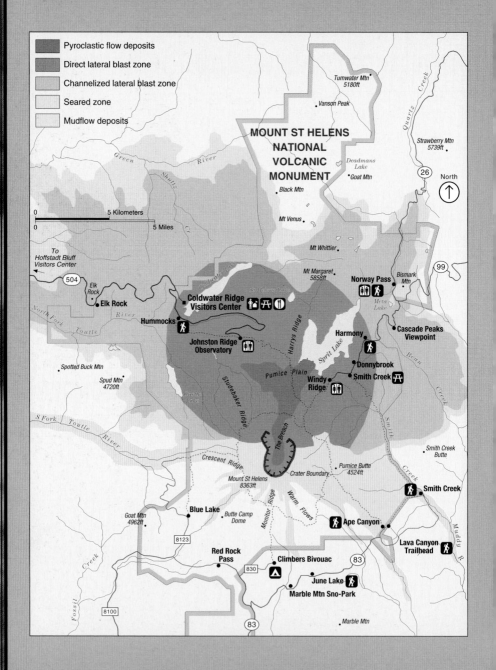

Pyroclastic flow deposits

Direct lateral blast zone

Channelized lateral blast zone

Seared zone

Mudflow deposits

Tumwater Mtn
5180ft

Vanson Peak

Quartz Creek

Strawberry Mtn
5739ft

**MOUNT ST HELENS
NATIONAL
VOLCANIC
MONUMENT**

Deadmans
Lake

Green River

Shalle Cr

Black Mtn

Goat Mtn

26

North

Mt Venus

5 Kilometers

0   5 Miles

To
Hoffstadt Bluff
Visitors Center

Mt Whittier

Mt Margaret
5858ft

Norway Pass

Bismark
Mtn

99

504

Elk
Rock

Elk Rock

North Fork

River

Toutle

Coldwater Ridge
Visitors Center

Harrys Ridge

Meta
Lake

Hummocks

Cascade Peaks
Viewpoint

Johnston Ridge
Observatory

Harmony

Spirit Lake

Spotted Buck Mtn

Pumice Plain

Donnybrook

Smith Creek

Spud Mtn
4720ft

Studebaker Ridge

Windy
Ridge

Bean Creek

S Fork   Toutle   River

The Breach

Smith Creek
Butte

Crescent Ridge

Crater Boundary

Pumice Butte
4524ft

Smith Creek

Mount St Helens
8363ft

Montior Ridge

Warm Flows

Smith Creek

Goat Mtn
4962ft

Blue Lake

Butte Camp
Dome

Ape Canyon

8123

Lava Canyon
Trailhead

Muddy R

Red Rock
Pass

Climbers Bivouac

830

83

Fossil Creek

8100

June Lake

Marble Mtn Sno-Park

83

Marble Mtn

MOUNT ST. HELENS
NATIONAL VOLCANIC MONUMENT

▸ **GETTING THERE**

Mount St. Helens National Volcanic Monument is in Southwestern Washington. Drive south from Seattle or north from Portland, Oregon, on Interstate 5 to Castle Rock, Washington. Turn east on Washington State Route 504 for 40 miles to the monument.

▸ **ESSENTIALS**

Entrance fees are collected year round. The road is open in winter when possible to Coldwater Ridge Visitor Center. At night, road remains open but the three excellent visitor centers—Silver Lake, Coldwater Ridge, and Johnston Ridge—close down. Food service is available, but not lodging, camping, or gasoline.

▸ **CLIMATE**

Generally warm in summer, but weather can change suddenly. Snow in winter, rainy in spring.

▸ **INFORMATION**

Mount St. Helens
National Volcanic Monument
3029 Spirit Lake Highway
Castle Rock, WA 98611
Telephone: 360 274-2100
Website: www.fs.fed.us/gpnf/mshnvm

▸ **VOLCANO FACTS**

Name – Mount Saint Helens
Volcano type –stratovolcano with lava
  dome in large crater
Rock types – basalt, andesite, and dacite
Height – 9,677 feet in 1979, reduced
  to 8,365 feet in 1980 eruption
Latest eruption – 1986

Top: Lying beyond the blast area just outside the monument boundary, Iron Creek Falls hints at the lush beauty that characterized the slopes of Mount St. Helens before the blast.
Above: Hikers climb to the viewpoint above Windy Ridge, northeast of Mount St. Helens.

LASSEN

VOLCANIC NATIONAL PARK, CALIFORNIA

Before Mount St. Helens startled the country with its huge and devastating 1980 eruption, Lassen Peak in California held the distinction of being the only volcano in the contiguous United States to erupt in the 20th century.

When activity began at Mount St. Helens, photographers from all over the world converged on Washington State, and nightly television news broadcasts were full of dramatic pictures of towering ash clouds above a shattered mountain, flattened forests and surging mudflows. But Lassen Peak's eruption happened before television was invented and even motion pictures were an oddity. The start of Lassen's eruption, which began in 1914 and continued sporadically for seven years, was documented largely by one man, a local businessman and amateur photographer named Benjamin F. Loomis.

The country around Lassen Peak was sparsely settled in 1914, so the first small steam explosions that started in late May of that year went almost unnoticed except by a few local ranchers, who thought a forest fire might be burning. Over the next week it became evident that the explosions were indeed coming from the volcano. No warning earthquakes had been felt, but a forest ranger who climbed to the summit discovered that a new crater had been excavated and was growing larger.

While other curious climbers reached the summit to see the new phenomenon, B.F. Loomis set up his camera on a tripod near Manzanita Lake in the expectation that something more dramatic was about to happen. He was not disappointed. On June 14, a dense, dark eruption cloud shot 2,500 feet into the sky. The heavier parts of the ash cloud fell back and rolled down the mountainside, engulfing and badly frightening a group of climbers. Loomis had his camera in an ideal spot, and his remarkable series of photos taken that day became justly famous.

Volcanic activity continued that summer with increasing intensity, enlarging the new crater to 1,000 feet in width. Ash clouds shot as high as 11,000 feet above Lassen Peak, and ash fell on the ranches and small towns on all sides of the mountain.

In May 1915, almost a year after the first eruptive activity, something new happened. A small dome of black, glassy lava pushed up into the crater. Loomis could see it from below, but could not decide

◄ *Opposite: Kings Creek meanders through a picture-perfect meadow in the foreground, and beyond, Lassen Peak rises above a forest-covered ridge. In summer the meadow is a wildflower garden of shooting stars, monkey flowers, lupine, pussy paws and countless others.*

▲ B.F. Loomis caught the initial stages of an eruption cloud roaring up from Lassen Peak in June 1914 at the start of a succession of explosive eruptions that continued intermittently until 1917.

what it was. Before anyone had time to inspect it closely, a huge explosion on the night of May 19 shattered the new dome and threw blocks of hot lava over the crater rim. The hot blocks fell on a steep snow slope, and a mixture of lava and snow avalanched down the east side of Lassen Peak. The heat melted large quantities of the deep snow, and mudflows swept down nearby creeks, putting many ranches in peril.

Two days later Loomis ventured into what is now called the Devastated Area, and found it completely barren except for mud, ash and some large lava blocks that were still hot to the touch. He set up his camera and took another series of photographs, including one of a group of onlookers standing beside a huge boulder that had been carried down in the avalanche; he labeled it "Hot Rock."

After he had used his last photographic plate that day he headed for home—a fortunate move. Just a few hours later another massive explosion from Lassen Peak sent a pyroclastic flow, a deadly cloud of hot lava fragments and gas, racing down the mountainside and engulfing the spot where he had stood. An eruption cloud rose to 25,000 feet above the volcano, and mudflows again inundated the creeks.

After this climactic eruption, activity began to wane. Small steam explosions happened now and then through 1917, and people reported puffs of steam as late as 1921, but Lassen Peak has been slumbering since then.

But Benjamin Loomis remained captivated by his mountain. Along with local Congressman John Raker, he successfully crusaded to have a bill passed in 1916 creating Lassen Volcanic National

Park. In 1926 Loomis and his wife bought a piece of privately owned land near Manzanita Lake and built a museum; a few years later they donated the land and picturesque rock building to the National Park Service. It is still in use as the Loomis Museum, showcasing his remarkable collection of photographs and other exhibits about the volcano.

Lassen Peak is the southernmost volcano in the Cascade chain, a line of 15 volcanoes stretching from British Columbia to Northern California. Almost all the other Cascade peaks are stratovolcanoes, steep-sided cones made up of layer upon layer of lava flows and ash deposits. Lassen Peak is different. It is a huge dome of lava, similar to the much smaller dome that is growing in the crater of Mount St. Helens. It is composed of dacite lava that was so thick and viscous when it erupted that it pushed up and solidified into a high mound over its vent instead of pouring down the mountainside as a lava flow. Lassen Peak is known as the world's largest plug dome volcano, a singularly unattractive name for a beautiful mountain.

Lassen Peak grew on the shoulder of an ancient stratovolcano that is often spoken of as Ancient Mount Tehama, or Brokeoff Volcano. That volcano had collapsed and eroded long before the present Lassen Peak started to grow, about 27,000 years ago.

Only about a thousand years ago a group of dacite lava domes were squeezed up on the north side of Lassen Peak, followed by a series of large explosive eruptions. These jagged peaks are known

▼ *This area north of Lassen Peak, today thickly mantled by a young conifer forest, was devastated when B.F. Loomis snapped this photograph following an eruption of May 20, 1915. The 300 ton boulder in the foreground was swept down from the summit by an avalanche and hot mudflow. This boulder took many months to cool, and is still known as Hot Rock.*

National Park Service

▲ **Above:** A steep trail spirals up the 700-foot-high Cinder Cone, located more than a mile from the nearest road in the remote northeast corner of the park. Scientists believe the cone was formed about AD 1650.

▼ **Below:** Boardwalks lead visitors safely past the steaming pools and bubbling mud pots of Bumpass Hell, the largest hot-spring area west of Yellowstone National Park. Located above 8,000 feet in elevation, the trail is sometimes closed by winter snows until well into August.

today as Chaos Crags. About 300 years ago great volumes of rock avalanched down from Chaos Crags, creating a chaotic deposit of broken rubble now called Chaos Jumbles and covering more than four square miles.

It is not clear what triggered the avalanche—perhaps a large earthquake, or a steam explosion that shattered one of the domes, or possibly the intrusion of another dome into the group, destabilizing the formation. In any case, it was an event that could happen again, and for several years the National Park Service posted "No Stopping" signs on the road through Chaos Jumbles.

Lassen Peak may look tranquil and permanent now, but the clearest clues that it is only fitfully sleeping can be seen in the bubbling, fuming thermal areas that dot the park. In these hydrothermal areas, groundwater is heated by slowly-cooling bodies of molten rock that have forced their way up but have not reached the surface. Above them, hot springs and fumaroles emit clouds of steam, carbon dioxide and pungent sulfur gases. Percolating hot, acid waters decompose rock to clay, and hot, wet clay turns to mud. The bubbling and boiling mud pots in these hot spring areas are fascinating to watch but keep your distance—they can be scalding.

Sulphur Works, right on Lassen's main road, has a boardwalk trail that leads through a hissing swirl of volcanic gases and around bubbling pools of mud. It is most important to stay on the trail; temperatures here have been measured at 195°F. Bumpass Hell is even

larger, the largest hot-spring area west of Yellowstone. An easy, three-mile (round trip) trail leads to this unearthly but beautiful series of boiling pools and streams, clouded with steam. The pools are eerie shades of blue and green, caused by thin layers of hot-water algae. The clay banks shade from pinks to yellows, stained by iron oxides. Other thermal areas that are well worth a visit if you have time for a side trip are Boiling Springs Lake and Devil's Kitchen in the south-eastern part of the park.

But the thermal features and the towering volcano are not the only stories at Lassen Volcanic National Park. For the visitor who expects to see a volcanic landscape of bare desolation, Lassen's dense forests and wildflower meadows come as a welcome surprise. The same recovery process that is taking place at Mount St. Helens is operating here, but with a 65-year head start. Besides the passage of time, there are two main reasons for the healthy and diverse plant growth. First, over time volcanic ash and rock disintegrate into deep, rich, fertile soils that support lush communities of plants. Secondly, Lassen lies where three provinces—the Cascade Range, the Sierra Nevada and the Great Basin—meet, so plants and trees from all three grow and flourish here. The flower-filled meadows, sparkling streams and water-falls, and tree-fringed lakes stand in quiet contrast to Lassen's hints of past and future volcanic violence, a clear reminder of the two faces of Nature.

▲ **Above:** *The background cliffs are known as Chaos Crags, dacite lava domes formed about a thousand year ago. In the foreground is Chaos Jumbles, created by a huge avalanche that swept from the Crags across this area about 300 years ago.*

▼ **Below:** *Part of a great spine of nearly solid rock thrust up by the growing lava dome, the eye-shaped scar is known as Vulcan's Eye.*

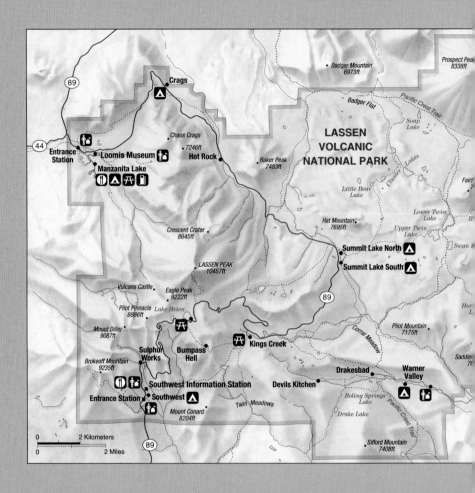

▸GETTING THERE

Lassen Volcanic National Park is located in Northern California, 50 miles east of Redding on State Highway 44. There are scheduled flights to Redding from San Francisco.

▸CLIMATE

Warm, generally dry days with cool nights prevail in summer. Snowstorms are common from November to April.

LASSEN
VOLCANIC NATIONAL PARK

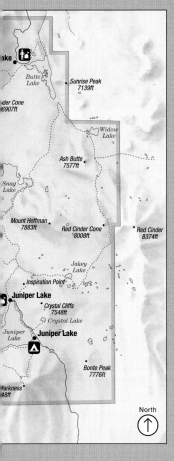

► **ESSENTIALS**

Entrance fees are charged when the park road is open, generally from mid-June to late October. The 29-mile road that crosses the park from north to south is closed by heavy winter snowfalls. There is food and lodging in summertime at Drakesbad Guest Ranch by reservation (530-529-9820), and food at Lassen Chalet and Manzanita Camper Store. Gasoline is also available at the Camper Store. The Loomis Museum at Manzanita Lake is open daily from mid-June through late September. Campgrounds and group campsites available.

► **INFORMATION**

Lassen Volcanic National Park
Post Office Box 100
Mineral, CA 96063
Telephone: 530-595-4444
Website: www.nps.gov/lavo

► **VOLCANO FACTS**

Name – Lassen Peak
Volcano type – lava dome
Rock type – dacite
Height – 10,457 feet
Latest eruption – 1914 to 1921

Above: Western wallflower.
At right: Marmot.

83

ANIAKCHAK
NATIONAL MONUMENT AND PRESERVE, ALASKA

Texans and Alaskans like to boast about their records—the biggest, the best, the most—but when it comes to the number of active volcanoes, Alaskans win hands down: Texas zero, Alaska more than forty that have erupted since Russian fur traders began keeping records in 1760. Aniakchak Volcano's latest eruption in 1931, and its spectacular caldera, put it high on the list of Alaska's great volcanoes. For a capsule description of Aniakchak Caldera, imagine Crater Lake in Oregon with a deep gash in its caldera wall that largely drains the lake.

▼ *An aerial view of Aniakchak's six-mile-wide, 2,000-foot-deep caldera shows its similarity to the more famous Crater Lake in Oregon, but with the lake largely drained away. Spectacular Aniakchak Caldera was created by an immense explosive eruption and collapse about 3,500 years ago. The volcanoes inside the caldera all formed by eruptions after the great explosion, the latest in 1931.*

Twelve cubic miles of pyroclastic deposits were spewed out from beneath Aniakchak Volcano in an enormous eruption about 3,500 years ago. The summit of the old 7,000-foot-high stratovolcano collapsed into the void below, creating Aniakchak Caldera—a nearly circular basin six miles wide and 2,000 feet deep, surrounded by steep cliffs. The high point remaining on the rim of the caldera is 4,398 feet, 3,300 feet above the caldera floor.

Aniakchak is near the middle of the Alaska Peninsula, 420 miles southwest of Anchorage. It is in a remote area known to humans for 8,000 years, but only "discovered" in 1922 when a geologic field

M. Williams, NPS

party peered down from the rim into the vast cliff-walled basin. Father Bernard Hubbard, a Jesuit Priest from Santa Clara University in California and an enthusiastic Alaska explorer, led a small group of students who trekked into the caldera for two weeks during the summer of 1930. His vivid descriptions in newspaper and magazine articles first called attention to this remarkable landscape.

In a September 1931 article in *National Geographic Magazine*, Hubbard describes his 1930 expedition as discovering "a world inside a mountain." He was amazed by the amount of life in the caldera where they had expected only the inside of a barren, sterile volcano. Although the tundra landscape was devoid of large trees, birds, foxes, hares, caribou and bears were abundant, while salmon and trout swam in small Surprise Lake on the floor of the caldera. Brown bears had worn deep tracks alongside the lake, and there was evidence they had even taken warm mud baths near active steam vents.

But in May 1931, a large explosive eruption from a vent within the caldera suddenly destroyed Father Hubbard's "paradise found." High ash columns spread grit as far as 150 miles away. Ash falling in

▲ *Above:* Geologists survey the volcanic scenery from the rim of Vent Mountain, a young stratovolcano within the caldera. They are looking toward Half Cone, a major explosive vent on the caldera floor.

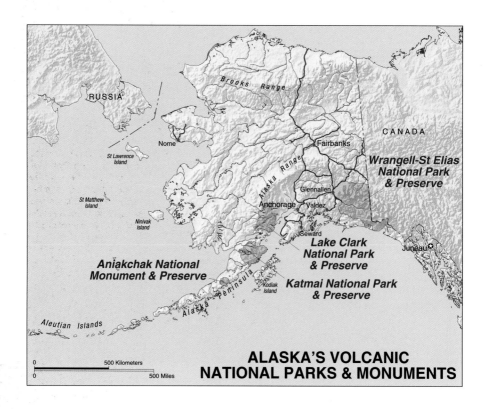

ALASKA'S VOLCANIC
NATIONAL PARKS & MONUMENTS

▲ The National Park Service manages 15 units in Alaska, nine of which are national parklands. Three of those parks and one monument labeled in this map contain a total of six live volcanoes that have erupted during the 20th century. More than 40 Alaskan volcanoes have erupted since 1760, when Russian fur traders began keeping records.

the village of Chignik and lumps of floating pumice "as big as buckets" disrupted the salmon industry. Hubbard returned with a new expedition, but now found "paradise lost."

From the caldera rim he saw "...the new Aniakchak, but it was the abomination of desolation.... Black walls, black floor, black water, deep black holes and black vents; it fairly agonized the eye to look at it.... There was a huge black crater built out from the wall, and from its black maw yellow and brown gases were pouring, and clouds of escaping steam."

But as seen at Mount St. Helens and Lassen, the Earth recovers with remarkable speed and vitality. Recent expeditions have again seen life and stark beauty return to Aniakchak. Lush fields of sedge, mare's tail and marigold near the lakeshore, and orchids bordering the warm springs were seen by James Sugar's expedition in the early 1980s before they rafted the rapids of the Aniakchak River that drains the caldera.

During the years and centuries that followed the immense prehistoric eruption, a large, 15-square-mile lake slowly filled the caldera to a depth of more than 300 feet. Evidence of that old lake was discovered by Game McGimsey of the U.S. Geological Survey in the early 1990s when he found wave-cut shoreline scars high on the caldera walls. At maximum depth, the lake surface reached just below the lowest point on the east side of the caldera rim. Later, possibly propelled by a sub-lake eruption, the lake spilled over the rim, generating a huge flood and quickly eroding a 2,000-foot canyon down into the caldera rim. Boulders as large as 100 feet long were swept down this deep gorge, now known as The Gates. The date of this catastrophic flood has not yet been established, but volcanic ash layers covering old lake-bottom sediments indicate it happened more than 500 years ago. Surprise Lake is the remnant of the large prehistoric lake that once filled Aniakchak Caldera.

Many volcanic features within the caldera have grown since the great eruption and collapse 3,500 years ago. Vent Mountain, a volcano inside a volcano, is a small stratovolcano in its own right, rising 3,350 feet above the caldera floor. Half Cone, a vent near the north wall, has apparently been the source of several explosive eruptions, including a violent one 500 years ago.

Amanda Austin

▲ **Above:** *Arctic Lupine.*

▼ **Below:** *Surprise Lake in Aniakchak Caldera is the source of the Aniakchak River, which exits the caldera through The Gates, a great cleft eroded in the caldera rim by floodwaters when the prehistoric lake overflowed.*

Tina Neal, also with the U.S. Geological Survey, has recently studied the lavas and ash beds from the Aniakchak eruptions. Her quick summary of Aniakchak includes the following: The huge caldera-forming eruption 3,500 years ago was mainly pyroclastic flows and ashfalls of dacite pumice erupted at a temperature of 1,560°F. The pyroclastic flows created an apron of thick deposits that reach as far as 35 miles beyond the caldera rim. Airborne ash fell as far as 900 miles away. At least 18 eruptions of andesite to dacite have happened since 3,500 years ago, some explosive and some lava flows. The 1931 eruption was composed of andesite bombs and dacite pumice airfall, with a rough total volume of .07 cubic miles. Along with her geologic discoveries, our friend Tina sent us some vivid memories of her field work at Aniakchak:

"Approaching Aniakchak Volcano by air you see miles and miles of relatively flat, featureless tundra. Suddenly the ground drops away and below you is this enormous crater, nearly a circular bowl enclosing a small blue-green lake, and classic volcanic landforms that look as though they could have formed yesterday. It is a breathtaking experience.

"To work inside Aniakchak means establishing a sturdy camp in a protected cove of Surprise Lake, nestled between lobes of blocky lava. The volcano is known for fierce winds and lashing rain, and clouds that pour down the cliffs like waterfalls. My colleague Game McGimsey and I learned the hard way that stabilizing a weatherport to withstand the Aniakchak blows means strong rope and deadmen and more rope and deadmen. After repairing one blown-out wall during our first stay, we never under-engineered a tent again.

"But we were fortunate enough to stay inside the crater long enough to see many gentle, long summer days as well, still and hot enough to bathe in the lake and marvel at the reflection of caldera walls on the glassy surface. Caribou and big brown bears were sometimes our neighbors in this lonely land. Game and I once watched an eagle swoop low over our heads to pluck a fox pup who had carelessly emerged from its den; the mother fox shrieked and ran helplessly after the big bird and we silently urged the remaining pup to get back inside.

"Although Aniakchak is in remote country, some 600 permanent residents live in small settlements within 100 miles of the volcano. If an eruption similar to the 1931 explosions were to happen again, it would severely impact life and commerce in Alaska—in the air as well as on the ground. On a clear day you can see contrails from dozens of large jet aircraft over the volcano flying the main passenger and trade route between North America and Asia."

At this time fewer than a hundred hardy travelers visit Aniakchak National Monument every year, but the same could have been said for Yellowstone National Park in 1874. No one knows what the next 125 years will bring, but one thing is sure: Wilderness will be important.

Top left: *Lupine.*
Below: *fireweed blossom.*

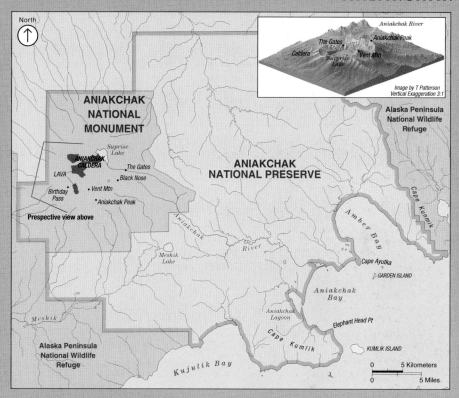

▸ GETTING THERE

Aniakchak National Monument is in Southern Alaska on the west end of the Alaska Peninsula. Fly to Anchorage, Alaska, then to King Salmon. Hire a float plane to land you in or near the monument. Be sure to make pick-up arrangements for the float plane to take you back out. A good way to see the caldera is to wait for a clear day in King Salmon and hire a light plane for an overflight.

▸ CLIMATE

Long, dark, cold, snowy winters, with some short periods of clear weather in the summer-time. Most summer days are overcast with temperatures in the high 40s or low 50s Fahrenheit, and major storms with high winds and rain may suddenly occur.

▸ ESSENTIALS

No fees or facilities.

▸ INFORMATION

Aniakchak National Monument
Post Office Box 7
King Salmon, AK 99613
Telephone: 907-246-3305
Website: www.nps.gov/ania

▸ VOLCANO FACTS

Name – Aniakchak

Volcano type – stratovolcano with caldera

Rock types – andesite and dacite

Height – 4,400 feet

Latest eruption – 1931

KATMAI

NATIONAL PARK AND PRESERVE, ALASKA

On a clear day in June 1912, the U.S. Revenue Steamship *Manning* was moored at the wharf in Kodiak, Alaska. At about four in the afternoon her skipper, Captain Perry, noticed a change in the sky. "I observed a peculiar-looking cloud...and remarked to a friend that it looked like snow. Later, distant thunder was heard, and about 5 P.M. I noticed light particles of ashes falling. At 6 o'clock the ashes fell in considerable showers, these gradually increasing. Thunder and lightning had become frequent at 7 o'clock, very intense at times, and though lacking two hours of sunset, a black night had settled down."

That black night was to last 60 hours while a foot of volcanic ash fell upon the terror-stricken fishing town of Kodiak, 100 miles downwind from an exploding volcano. Which volcano? No one in the blackout of Kodiak had the slightest idea. The mystery was solved by the captain of another ship, the *Dora,* that was steaming eastbound through the Shelikof Strait between the Alaska Peninsula and Kodiak. Captain McMullen recorded in his log: "Left Uyak at 8:45 A.M., June 6; strong westerly breeze and fine clear weather. At 1 o'clock P.M., while entering Kupreanoff Straits, sighted a heavy cloud of smoke directly astern, rising from the Alaska Peninsula. I took bearings of the same, which I made out to be Katmai Volcano, distance about 55 miles away."

The *Dora* tried to reach Kodiak, its next mail stop, but by 7 P.M. had to head out to sea to avoid the blinding and near-suffocating fall of ashes. Captain McMullen noted they were in "...complete darkness, not even the water over the ships side could be seen." A mail clerk who was aboard, was quoted later in the Seward newspaper, noting, "The officers of the deck had to close the windows of the pilot-house tightly, and even then it was with the greatest difficulty that the man at the wheel could see the compass, through the thick dust that filled the room. Below deck conditions were unbearable, while on deck it was worse still. Dust filled our nostrils, sifted down our backs, and smote the eye like a dash of acid. Birds floundered, crying wildly, ...and fell helpless to the deck."

The 800 inhabitants of Kodiak endured severe headaches, sore eyes and pain in the throat and lungs from the 60-hour ashfall. Two or three people died, but their deaths were considered hastened by

◄ *Opposite:*
Trident Volcano, a near neighbor of Mount Katmai, erupted intermittently from 1953 to 1974. When this photograph was taken in 1963, the cone of this complex volcano had reached 800 feet above the surrounding area, and its steaming crater was about 500 feet wide. Fumaroles on the crater rim were depositing sulfur and their temperature exceeded 400° F., the limit of the authors' thermometer.

▲ *The Valley of Ten Thousand Smokes as seen by Robert Griggs. The steaming valley was created in 1912 by a thick pyroclastic flow deposit from Novarupta Volcano. The eruption from Novarupta and the collapse of Mount Katmai was the world's largest volcanic event of the 20th century. Fumaroles of steam from water boiling out of the hot pyroclastic deposit produced the thousands of "smokes."*

the ordeal and not due primarily to the eruption. Because the area closer to Mount Katmai was nearly uninhabited, and the few that lived there were frightened away by the preceding earthquakes, apparently no one was killed by the world's largest volcanic eruption of the 20th century.

The total ashfall in the town of Kodiak was close to one foot, but drifts were thicker where blown by the wind, and much thicker where the loose ash slid down steep hillsides into piles at their base. Buildings close to these avalanches of ash were partly crushed and buried. Gardens were covered, pastures were buried, fishing was disrupted, but through pluck and courage, the town survived. The western half of Kodiak Island received very little ashfall. As it was summertime, many people from the town of Kodiak moved there temporarily while the settlement was digging out.

The U.S. Geological Survey and the National Geographic Society mounted an expedition to learn more about the great eruption, sending geologist George Martin to investigate. He arrived in Kodiak from Washington DC in July 1912.

Although bad weather and the thick, loose ash, up to five feet thick on the coast of the Shelikof Strait 15 miles from the volcano, prevented Martin from reaching Mount Katmai, he made an excellent preliminary map of the ashfall. By interviewing many witnesses, he pieced together a good chronology of the eruption. In Kodiak he observed that the ashfall had three distinct layers: a bottom layer of coarse gray ash four inches thick, followed by five inches of fine brown ash, and a two-inch top layer of fine white ash. These observations were significant to later scientists who have worked out the timing and nature of events that were involved in this complex and mighty eruption. George Martin estimated the total volume of the ashfall at five cubic miles. It was that estimate, which has generally stood the test of later, more detailed investigations, that established the Katmai eruption as the 20th century's largest.

The next major expedition on the scene was sponsored by the National Geographic Society and led by botanist Robert Griggs of Ohio State University. Griggs, interested in how vegetation recovers from a volcanic eruption, made a brief visit to Kodiak in the summer of 1913, but his summer explorations on and near Mount Katmai were made in 1915, 1916, 1917, and 1919. His amazing discoveries and vivid accounts in the *National Geographic Magazine* led to the establishment of Katmai National Monument in 1918.

▼ *Three members of the 1916 Griggs Expedition are dwarfed by Katmai's vast volcanic landscape. Wrote one member of the next expedition to behold this scene: "The meager pictures of the previous year...had not prepared me to face such a spectacle of awesome magnitude. I had pictured the Valley as large; the actual view dwarfed my wildest imagery to insignicance."*

National Geographic Society.

When Griggs first visited Kodiak, a year after the eruption, he noted that it appeared barren and desolate. He and most of the remaining residents thought it would be many years before "Green Kodiak" recovered. Returning in the summer of 1916, Griggs was astounded by the change. Fields of grass "as high as one's head" replaced barren ash. Townspeople all agreed the eruption was "the best thing that ever happened in Kodiak"—green grass for pastures, lush gardens, huge berries, and great fishing.

But like Martin's, Griggs's small, three-man expedition was hampered by the thick ash deposits and quicksand-filled streams as they tried to explore the southern flanks of Mount Katmai, where vegetation had not recovered. High fans of loose ash that had avalanched from the steep mountain sides, and wide ash-and-pumice-filled streams "five miles wide and five inches deep" impeded their explorations. They did, however, sight four great steaming volcanoes: Mount Katmai and Mount Megeik, already known and charted, and two new ones—Mount Martin and Trident Volcano. It was evident the top of Mount Katmai was missing, but they were not able to climb to the remnant summit.

Nineteen-sixteen was the year of discovery for Griggs and his three companions. They reached the rim of Katmai Crater and were not disappointed. As the swirling steam cleared, "...we were struck speechless by the scene, for the whole crater lay before us. It was of immense size and seemed an infinite depth. Almost half the bottom was occupied by a wonderful blue and green vitriolic lake. Around the margin were a thousand jets of steam of all sizes, issuing from every crevice with a roar like a great locomotive...." After a second climb to the rim ten days later, Griggs estimated the length of the crater at three miles and its depth to be to be at least 2,000 feet.

▲ **Above:** *A lone fumarole and collapse pit near Novarupta lava dome was one of the few "smokes" left in 1963.*

During their climbs, members of the expedition noticed wisps of clouds or steam from the north side of the volcanic range. Determined to learn their source, Griggs and Folsom crossed Katmai Pass between Trident and Megeik Volcanoes, and were amazed to discover an entire valley filled with steaming fumaroles. In Griggs words: "...the whole valley as far as the eye could reach was full of hundreds, no thousands—literally, tens of thousands—of smokes curling up from its fissured floor."

Lured onward they also discovered the steaming lava dome which Griggs later named "Novarupta." He correctly interpreted this feature to be "...a plug of lava being slowly pushed up through a vent which was formerly rather violently explosive...." His first interpretation that the Valley of Ten Thousand Smokes was underlain by a great volcanic fissure extending from Katmai Pass for many miles towards Naknek Lake is no longer accepted. It is now known to be a thick pyroclastic-flow deposit that issued from Novarupta. Nevertheless, the discoveries

▼ **Below:** *A lake fills the caldera created in 1912 by the removal of magma from beneath the summit of Mount Katmai. The astounding fact of the Novarupta eruption is that it is six miles away from the caldera. Early explorers assumed much of the erupted material came from Katmai Volcano, but later, more detailed examinations indicate that almost all the huge ashfall and pyroclastic flow deposits came from Novarupta.*

Tina Neal, USGS

George Wuerthner

▲ A hiker gingerly examines an erosional canyon in the floor of the Valley of Ten Thousand Smokes. The canyon provides a window into the layers of the ash-flow deposit that filled the original valley to a depth of up to 700 feet in places.

of Griggs, Folsom, and Church were prodigious: Katmai Crater, Martin, Trident, and Novarupta Volcanoes, and the famous Valley of Ten Thousand Smokes. They revealed the amazing features of one of the world's greatest volcanic eruptions, and were rewarded with support for a larger expedition in the summer of 1917.

Ten men made up this new expedition including a topographer to map the region and a chemist to analyze the gases from the fumaroles. Strangely, no geologist made the team. Mr. Maynard, the topographer, did not share Professor Griggs's enthusiasm for Katmai. He wrote, "The smokes did not impress me with their grandeur or with their wonder as natural phenomena. Their ability to make surveying next to impossible did.... On the few rare days when it was not raining and the wind was not doing its best to move our camp (rather good judgement on the part of the wind, I should say) they would shoot forth jets of steam which soon took the form of clouds and obscured the country we were trying to work.... the coming of the smokes ruined what might otherwise have been perfectly good country. My opinion, however, is probably valueless, as being out of tobacco always colors my views."

Mr. Shipley, the chemist, was not quite so critical in his account. "On first entering the valley between the two guardian volcanic cones, I experienced the same sensation as the man who on seeing a giraffe for the first time exclaimed, 'There ain't no such animal'.... It is so unreal. Hot streams flow from beneath banks of snow; extensive glaciers hobnob with steaming fumaroles, while icebergs and hot water are found in the same little lake. Enormous mud-flows appear to run uphill [later interpreted by geologists to be pyroclastic flows]. A stick chars when thrust into a jet of steam.... The familiar fumes of hydrogen sulphide, sulphur dioxide, and hydrochloric acid transform the valley into a large chemical manufacturing plant roofed over by a permanent cloud of vapors."

Despite the hardships of collecting data in this harsh environment, the 1917 expedition made several important observations. Novarupta was recognized as an important vent of large quantities of ash and pumice, but was still thought to be secondary to Mount Katmai. The Valley of Ten Thousand Smokes was determined to be 13 miles long and two to six miles wide. Katmai Crater was measured at more than two miles wide, 8.4 miles in circumference, and a maximum of 3,700 feet deep from the highest point on the rim to the crater lake. Its volume including the missing summit was estimated to be two cubic miles.

Griggs returned again in 1919. The number of "smokes" had diminished, but some still emitted gases at temperatures above 1,000°F. By this time he realized that the valley had been filled by a seething hot pyroclastic flow which he called an incandescent sand flow. He considered the source of the flow to be Novarupta and fissures beneath the valley, but he still believed that Katmai had been the source of the huge ashfalls.

That interpretation held until the 1950s when Professors Howel Williams and Garniss Curtis of the University of California, mapped the distribution and thickness of the ash layers and determined that most of them came from Novarupta as well. By that time most of

▼ *Geologists hike toward 7,602-foot-high Mount Griggs. Fumaroles on the summit of Mount Griggs, named for the leader of the first scientific expedition to the Valley of Ten Thousand Smokes, indicate that this volcano is still active even though it has not erupted in recorded history.*

Game McGimsey, USGS

▲ Trident Volcano is composed of a cluster of five stratovolcanoes. Named Trident by Griggs, who only saw three summits (four are visible in this photo), its 1953 to 1974 eruption added the fifth. The lava dome of Novarupta, a low hill seen in the foreground, plugs the vent of the great 1912 eruption.

the fumaroles, except for some near Novarupta, had ceased steaming. Curtis concluded that Novarupta was the principal vent of both the ash explosions and the pyroclastic flow that filled the valley to depths of several hundred feet. Thus, the fumaroles in the valley have no roots below the originally hot, 1,500°F. pyroclastic flow. Most of the steam came from surface and groundwater that was covered by the hot flow, or from rainfall and runoff that seeped into the flow boiling back out.

In addition, Curtis and Williams concluded that the missing volume of Mount Katmai could be accounted for by collapse as magma was withdrawn from beneath it. This was an astounding idea, that an exploding volcanic vent could tap its magma source from beneath a volcano six miles away, or that an even larger magma chamber extended beneath both Novarupta and Katmai.

The most recent studies over many seasons of field work by Wes Hildreth and Judy Fierstein of the U.S. Geological Survey basically concur with Curtis's views, and have added a great deal of important data on the source, timing, volumes and compositions of the volcanic materials poured out during the great eruption. Their studies indicate that, except for a small lava dome that is now submerged beneath the lake in Katmai Caldera, all the erupted materials in 1912—nearly seven cubic miles—came from Novarupta. The ash cloud reached heights of about 20 miles and was followed by and partly overlapped in time with the pyroclastic flow that formed the ash-flow sheet in the Valley of Ten Thousand Smokes. The volume of the ashfalls is about 4.1 cubic miles, and the pyroclastic-flow volume is about 2.7 cubic miles.

Hildreth and Fierstein's recently published summary report on the great eruption adds new interpretations on the origin and source of the three cubic miles of magma expelled during the 60-hour-long eruption. (Note that the volume of magma is less than the combined volume of the lower-density ashfalls and ash-flow sheet.) The early hours of the eruption produced entirely rhyolite, followed later by mixtures of rhyolite, dacite, and andesite. Overall the eruptive products consist of 55 percent rhyolite, 35 percent dacite, and 10 percent andesite. The eruption apparently tapped a layered magma chamber beneath Mount Katmai, whose less-dense upper layer was entirely rhyolitic. They conclude that this, the largest eruption of rhyolite in the world during the past 1,800 years, was mainly formed by crystal fractionation.

Besides the giant eruption of Novarupta and the collapse of Katmai Caldera, there is one additional live volcano—Trident—and twelve sleeping volcanoes in Katmai National Park and Preserve. These last, that have erupted during the past 100,000 years, are (from southwest to northeast): Alagogshak, Mount Martin, Mount Megeik, Mount Griggs, Snowy Mountain, Mount Denison, Mount Steller, Kukak Volcano, Devils Desk, Kaguyak Crater, Fourpeaked Mountain, and Mount Douglas.

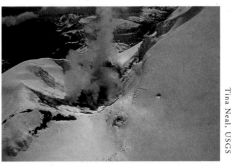

Tina Neal, USGS

▲ Above:
Vigorous fumaroles and a steaming hot lake occur near the snow-covered summit of 7,103 foot Mount Mageik. Plumes of vapor from this area are often mistaken for eruptions of Mageik.

▼ Below:
Sulfur deposits stain the snow- and ice-covered summit of Mount Martin, another sleeping volcano in the Katmai area. Future eruptions from volcanoes in this park are likely to occur in the next hundred years. This is a safe prediction for geologists who will not live long enough to see it disproved.

Tina Neal, USGS

Tom Miller, USGS

▲ *The rugged 250-foot-high lava dome in the center of the photo plugs the vent of Novarupta Volcano, whose 1912 eruption was the largest in the world in the 20th century. Seven cubic miles of falling ash and pyroclastic-flow deposits spewed from this vent in just 60 hours. Falling Mountain and Mount Mageik (in the far distance) are seen directly behind Novarupta.*

Trident Volcano, named by Griggs in 1915 for the three summits he could see, erupted intermittently from 1953 to 1974, giving Trident a fifth summit. After an explosive ash eruption in 1953 that a passing pilot compared to the mushroom cloud of an atomic bomb, Trident's new vent produced a succession of thick, viscous, blocky lava flows of andesite and dacite, and a summit cone more than 800 feet high.

Peter Ward (then a student of mine at Dartmouth) and I (Robert Decker) climbed this new cone during the summer of 1963 while we were doing seismic and gravity studies at Katmai. The crater was about 500 feet in diameter and completely obscured by thick steam and gases. Active solfataras encrusted with molten and crystalline sulfur covered the entire crater rim, and most of them were hotter than the 400°F. range of our thermometer. Small lava dome emplacements and explosions within the crater continued until 1974.

Katmai Pass separates Trident Volcano from Mount Megeik, a largely ice-covered volcano with four summits, the highest at 7,250 feet. A steam plume often rises from Megeik, but no known eruptions have occurred there during the 20th century. A four-mile-long landslide containing large boulders tumbled southeast from Megeik into the valley of Martin Creek during the 1912 eruption of Novarupta.

Mount Martin, four miles southwest of Megeik, is a 6,050-foot-high volcano that often vents a vigorous steam plume, but no known eruptions have occurred there during the 20th century. The steam plumes from Martin sometimes rise to nearly 2,000 feet, and have been incorrectly reported as ash eruptions.

Besides the obvious attraction of such beautiful landscapes and so many spectacular volcanic features in Katmai National Park and Preserve, the next most interesting features—even to a volcano lover—are the brown bears and the salmon. The huge brown bears, weighing up to a thousand pounds, are essentially giant grizzly bears. Fortunately they are less aggressive than their generally smaller but more violent cousins in the interior of Alaska—possibly because they are more well-fed on salmon. When Peter Ward and I spent the summer of 1963 at Katmai, we saw several of these huge bears. We avoided them, sometimes walking extra miles when we could see one far ahead. Thankfully, they also avoided us. A few times we saw them standing in the middle of a stream throwing salmon out on the bank until the pile was big enough for lunch.

Millions of two-foot-long salmon return to the streams and lakes in Katmai National Park and Preserve to spawn and die. Sometimes there are so many in the clear, shallow water that it appears bright red, and it seems so packed with salmon that you could walk across on a barely-submerged raft of fish. When hatched, the tiny young salmon swim to the ocean. When grown to adults they return to their birthplace—one of Nature's many wheels within wheels. The cycle of volcanic destruction and creation is a larger wheel, but still small within the marvel of our dynamic Earth.

▼ *The great brown bears at Katmai, though the same species as the more aggressive grizzlies farther north in Alaska, are well fed on salmon but still dangerous and unpredictable. Leave their portrait photos to an expert– or use a telephoto lens.*

Don Pitcher

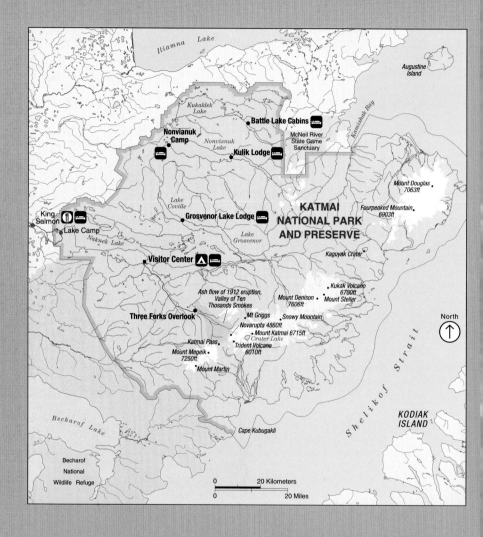

KATMAI
NATIONAL PARK AND PRESERVE

▶ **GETTING THERE**

Katmai National Park is located in Southern Alaska on the Alaska Peninsula. Fly to Anchorage, Alaska, then on to King Salmon. Reserve a float plane well in advance to fly into Brooks Camp Visitor Center on Naknek Lake. In summer, float planes generally fly daily between King Salmon and Brooks Camp. The best way to see the volcanoes is to wait for a clear day in King Salmon and hire a light plane for an overflight.

▶ **ESSENTIALS**

There is food and lodging (by reservation) at Brooks Lodge and Grosvenor Lake Lodge in summer. A bus from Brooks Camp makes a daily round trip (fee) to Three Forks Overlook on a 23-mile-long dirt road. The overlook is near the lower end of the Valley of Ten Thousand Smokes. The campground and visitor center at Brooks Camp is open in summer and early fall.

▶ **CLIMATE**

In summer, clear skies occur only about 20 percent of the time. Be prepared for rain and high winds. Daytime temperatures range in the 50s to 60s Fahrenheit with nighttime lows in the 40s.

▶ **INFORMATION**

Katmai National Park
Post Office Box 7
King Salmon, AK 99613
Telephone: 907-246-3305
Website: www.nps.gov/katm

▶ **VOLCANO FACTS**

Name – Katmai
Volcano type – stratovolcano with caldera
Rock types – andesite and dacite;
some basalt and rhyodacite
Height – about 7,500 feet prior to 1912
collapse, now 6,715 feet
Latest eruption – 1912

Name – Novarupta
Volcano type – lava dome in main vent
of the great 1912 eruption
Rock types – rhyolite, dacite, and andesite
Height – 200 feet above surrounding
ash-flow deposit
Latest eruption – 1912

Name – Trident
Volcano type – complex cluster
of stratovolcanoes
Rock types – andesite and dacite
Height – 6,115 feet
Latest eruptions –1953 to 1974

Don Pitcher

LAKE CLARK
NATIONAL PARK AND PRESERVE, ALASKA

Lake Clark National Park, the Alps of Alaska, has something the European Alps don't have: two great volcanoes, one very much alive, the other barely sleeping. Redoubt Volcano (10,197 feet) erupted in 1902, from 1966 to 1968, and again from 1989 to 1990. Iliamna Volcano (10,016 feet) had several reported eruptions during the 20th century, but experts on Alaskan volcanoes consider that these reports were probably caused by steam emissions from fumaroles high on the flank of the volcano, rather than by true eruptions.

With more than 6,000 square miles, Lake Clark National Park and Preserve takes its name from a 50-mile-long lake, an essential spawning area for sockeye salmon. The Chigmit Mountains include the two volcanoes, and separate the lake from Cook Inlet with a wild range of jagged peaks and grinding glaciers. The park is road-less, heaven to dedicated wilderness hikers. Exploring parties most often spend days without seeing another expedition. Access to the park is by boat or light aircraft. Float planes may land on the lakes,

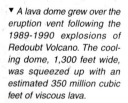

▼ A lava dome grew over the eruption vent following the 1989-1990 explosions of Redoubt Volcano. The cooling dome, 1,300 feet wide, was squeezed up with an estimated 350 million cubic feet of viscous lava.

Game McGimsey, USGS

ski planes on the snow-covered glaciers, and large-wheeled planes on open beaches or small private airstrips. The way to see these volcanoes is to wait for good weather and then take a light-plane flight from Anchorage, Homer or Kenai.

Redoubt Volcano awoke from a 21-year slumber on December 14 and 15, 1989, with four major explosive eruptions. The largest of those initial jetting explosions began at 10:15 on the morning of December 15. It lasted 40 minutes and lofted an ash cloud to 40,000 feet, where high speed winds carried it northeast.

At 11:45 a.m. that ash cloud, then 150 miles downwind from Redoubt, struck terror into 231 passengers and 13 crew members of a Boeing 747 that was arriving in Anchorage on a polar flight from Amsterdam. Weather was overcast as the pilot descended on instruments towards the airport. At 25,000 feet the plane entered the dark ash cloud buried in the general overcast. Realizing something was wrong, the pilot tried to climb just as the volcanic ash particles clogged and shut down all four engines. In agonizing silence and darkness for the next eight minutes, the jumbo jet glided 18,000 feet downward toward the mountainous terrain around Anchorage while the pilots struggled to restart the engines. With only 6,000 feet and three minutes left, the engines finally whined back into life, carrying the plane to a safe landing.

▲ *Above:Continuous, low-level eruption of ash and steam from Redoubt Volcano in December 1989 followed its initial large explosions. When a jumbo jet bound for Anchorage encountered the high ash cloud, hidden in storm clouds, all four engines were clogged and stopped by the ash-laden air, and the jet began a steep, potentially fatal, descent. Moments before it was too late the pilots were able to restart the engines.*

▶ *Overleaf:Photographer Robert Clucas captured Redoubt Volcano's spectacular eruption cloud on April 21, 1990, from across Cook Inlet on the Kenai Peninsula.* USGS

USGS

Examination of the engines revealed both the problem that near-ly downed the 747, and the emergency measures that saved it. Ash particles swept into the hot, operating engines were melted into glassy coatings on the engine turbines. Air intake was reduced by this clogging and the engines stopped. By gliding beneath the ash cloud into clearer air, the glass coatings chilled and cracked, and were partly broken off by the repeated tries to restart the engines. Enough air intake was finally reestablished to succeed. Replacing the damaged engines, the "ashblasted" windshields and leading edges of the wings, as well as a complete overhaul of the aircraft, cost $80 million—a costly accident but fortunately not a deadly one.

Can this type of near-fatal accident be avoided? Yes, by locating a volcanic ash cloud with ground-based sensors and satellite surveil-lance, and issuing real-time warnings to pilots of its whereabouts. It often takes a close call like this to get the process going.

Another near-tragedy caused by the Redoubt eruption was a close encounter with a major oil spill. The Drift River oil-storage tanks located 20 miles northeast of the volcano, collect petroleum piped

▲ **Above:** As seen from the Kenai Peninsula at sunset. Iliamna Volcano rises to 10,016 feet above the Cook Inlet.

◀ **Opposite:** The glacier carved, sleeping stratovol-cano, Iliamna, looms before travelers who approach the park by plane.

in from well platforms in the Cook Inlet, holding it for reloading into tankers. Large mudflows caused by the initial volcanic explosions in December 1989, and by the collapse of a newly-formed lava dome on Redoubt in January 1990, swept down the Drift River to the Cook Inlet. Rapidly melting glaciers high on the flank of the volcano provided the flood waters that propelled the mudflows. Although the oil terminal sustained some damage, the levees, built around the tanks to keep the oil in, kept the mudflows out. Oil storage during the initial mudflow totaled 800,000 barrels, but had been reduced before the larger January event.

Growth of new lava domes, and explosions that destroyed them, continued into April 1990. After that a final dome grew at a diminishing rate until mid-summer 1990, when the eruption of Redoubt Volcano was apparently over. As is often the case with a volcanic eruption, the time it starts is much easier to define than the time it stops.

Both Redoubt and Iliamna are stratovolcanoes, although Iliamna, because it consists of four peaks along a three-mile ridge, could also be called a complex volcano. Even though both volcanoes are still active, neither has the classic stratovolcano shape of

▼ A hiker on the ridge above Lake Clark enjoys a bit of shirt-sleeve weather, a welcome respite from the park's frequent summer rains. Visitors should be well prepared for extreme weather in the Alaskan backcountry.

George Wuerthner

Mount Fuji in Japan because glaciers are actively scouring them down. In the cold, snowy climate of 60 degrees north latitude, several mountain glaciers grind down the flanks of both volcanoes.

Redoubt and Iliamna are estimated to be about one million years old. Both are dominantly composed of andesite, but Redoubt has also erupted basalt and dacite. Lava flows and domes have built the steep summits of both volcanoes, while ashfall, pyroclastic-flow and mudflow deposits dominate their less-steep lower flanks. The hazards posed by these two volcanoes were aptly demonstrated by the costly 1989-1990 eruption of Redoubt, estimated to total $160 million. Fortunately no one was killed. Some danger always accompanies beautiful mountain country, but the beauty far outweighs the dangers.

Unspoiled wilderness awaits discovery by the hardy adventurers who visit Lake Clark National Park. Flight-seers, kayakers, hikers, mountain climbers, fishing enthusiasts, and wildlife watchers will all be amply rewarded if they have the patience and perseverance of true nature lovers.

▲ *The cone of 10,197 foot-high Redoubt Volcano has been severely eroded by mountain glaciers. Ash-laden explosions have occurred from Redoubt in 1902, 1966, 1967-68, and 1989-90. Pyroclastic flows during the 1989-90 eruptions melted large volumes of snow and ice and released major mudflows down the Drift River.*

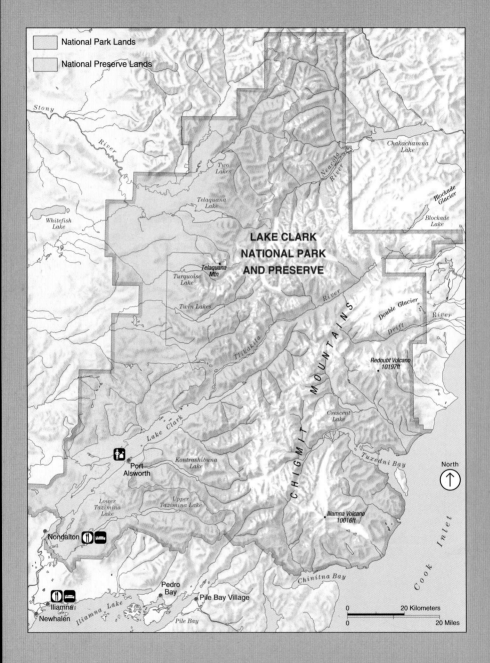

National Park Lands

National Preserve Lands

Stony River

Two Lakes

Neacola River

Chakachamna Lake

Telaquana Lake

Blockade Glacier

Whitefish Lake

Blockade Lake

**LAKE CLARK
NATIONAL PARK
AND PRESERVE**

Telaquana Mtn

Turquoise Lake

Twin Lakes

Tlikakila River

CHIGMIT MOUNTAINS

Double Glacier

Drift River

Redoubt Volcano
10197ft

Lake Clark

Crescent Lake

Kontrashibuna Lake

Port Alsworth

Tuxedni Bay

North

Lower Tazimina Lake

Upper Tazimina Lake

Illamna Volcano
10016ft

Nondalton

Cook Inlet

Pedro Bay

Pile Bay Village

Iliamna
Newhalen

Iliamna Lake

Chinitna Bay

Pile Bay

| 0 | | 20 Kilometers |
| 0 | | 20 Miles |

LAKE CLARK
NATIONAL PARK AND PRESERVE

▶ GETTING THERE

Lake Clark National Park is located in Southern Alaska on the north side of Cook Inlet. Fly to Anchorage, Alaska, and then fly or drive to Kenai or Homer. Access to the park is by boat, float plane, or large-wheeled light plane. The park is also accessible from the southwest via the town of Iliamna, itself linked to Anchorage by scheduled flight. A good way to see the volcanoes is to wait for a clear day in Kenai and hire a light plane for an overflight.

▶ ESSENTIALS

Field headquarters for the park are at Port Alsworth on Lake Clark. There are no other facilities, and no fees to enter the park.

▶ CLIMATE

Near the Cook Inlet daytime summer temperatures average in the 50s and 60s Fahrenheit, with lots of rain. To the northwest, away from Cook Inlet, the weather is warmer and drier, but frost occurs on some evenings. Winters are cold and dark.

▶ INFORMATION

Lake Clark National Park and Preserve
4230 University Drive, Suite 311
Anchorage, AK 99508
Telephone: 907-271-3751
Website: www.nps.gov/lacl

▶ VOLCANO FACTS

Name – Iliamna
Volcano type – stratovolcano
Rock type – andesite
Height – 10,016 feet
Latest eruption – ?

Name – Redoubt
Volcano type – stratovolcano
Rock type – andesite
Height – 10,197 feet
Latest eruption – 1989 to 1990

G. Gardner,USGS

Mudflow deposits from the 1989-90 eruption of Redoubt Volcano cover the wide valley floor of the Drift River.

WRANGELL-ST.ELIAS
NATIONAL PARK AND PRESERVE, ALASKA

Alaska not only has the distinction of having the most volcanoes of any of the 50 US states, it also has the largest national park. At 20,625 square miles, Wrangell-St. Elias is six times the size of Yellowstone. Mount Wrangell, 14,163 feet high, erupted steam and reworked ash in the early 1900s, and small steam bursts occurred as recently as the 1970s . That makes it the tallest live volcano in the United States. Nearby Mount St. Elias, although not a volcano, reaches 18,008 feet and is the fourth highest mountain in North America.

This great park, often called "the mountain kingdom," is the meeting ground of four major northwest-southeast trending ranges: the east end of the Alaska Range in the north, the Chugach Mountains on the south, the Wrangell Mountains in the center, and the St. Elias Mountains on the southeast. Icefields cap the higher elevations, and massive mountain glaciers carve deep canyons in the flanks of the ranges. It is a land of rugged, spectacular beauty, seemingly endless mountains, and the kind of country that earns Alaska its reputation as the last frontier.

As we learned at Katmai and Denali National Parks, the way to see and appreciate the scale and grandeur of Alaskan mountains is by light plane. In a two-hour flight from one of the airports near Wrangell-St. Elias National Park you take in more volcanic and glacial scenery than you can see in three summer field expeditions on the ground.

The geologic history of Wrangell-St. Elias National Park is much more complicated than the relatively simple subduction zone where the Aleutian Islands and the Alaska Peninsula mark the convergence of the Pacific Plate as it moves northwestward into Alaska. Here in Southeast Alaska, great segments of North America that were sheared off by strike-slip faults from areas much farther south have piled up into one another in complex mountains that geologists call "accreted terranes." These huge segments of land and seafloor have been slowly transported northward along ancient faults similar to today's San Andreas Fault in California. The Wrangellia terrane was originally an island arc (like Japan) that grew from about 300 to 200 million years ago in an area that is now California and off-shore

◀ *Opposite:*
Autumn settles into the forests of Wrangell-St. Elias by late August and early September, passing quickly, but spectacularly, into winter. Although typical of this latitude, the long days of summer and the long winter nights in Alaska might be disorienting to visitors from lower latitudes, but fall presents a happy median.

▲ *Volcanoes of the Wrangell Mountains include the 16,237-foot-high sleeping giant, Mount Sanford (left), and 14,163-foot-high Mount Wrangell. Both are andesitic shield volcanoes, a rare mix of rock type and shape. Most shield volcanoes are basaltic with more fluid lavas that tend to build their gently sloping sides.*

waters west of Mexico. Over the next 100 million years it was slowly moved northwestward as part of the Pacific Plate, ending (for the present) its long journey by being joined (accreted) to Alaska and Western Canada about 100 million years ago. Another slice followed later, part of which is now the Chugach Range. Next came the Yakutat Terrane which was added to Southeast Alaska about 25 million years ago.

To put this piling-up of accreted terranes into perspective, imagine the San Andreas Fault continuing to shear the Coast Range of California between Los Angeles and San Francisco northwestward for the next 100 million years. That would eventually add a huge segment of California to the south coast of Alaska. In human time the Earth's geography appears fixed and static; in geologic time the dance of the plates continually rearranges the patterns of oceans and continents that we know today.

But this is background. Where do the live, sleeping, and dead volcanoes of the Wrangell Mountains fit into this geologic scheme? Don Richter of the U.S. Geological Survey has studied the Wrangell Mountains for the past three decades. Most of the geologic information in this chapter is summarized from his guidebook listed at the end of this book.

Volcanoes began to grow in the Wrangell area about 26 million years ago, apparently caused by the subduction that accompanied accretion of the Yakutat Terrane. Although eruptions may now be waning in vigor, surprises could still be in store. Overall the Wrangell volcanic field extends from Alaska into the northwest end of the St. Elias Mountains in Canada. Its lavas cover 4,000 square miles in a northwest-southeast trending area 180 miles long and 20 to 70 miles wide.

Most subduction-related volcanoes in the world erupt explosively and build stratovolcanoes. The Wrangell volcanoes are exceptions; they erupt mainly lava flows and build shield volcanoes. The reasons for this contrary habit are not clear, but may be related to the eruption rate and complexity of the geology in this region of accreted terranes.

Ten tall volcanoes include Mount Sanford (16,237 feet), Mount Drum (12,010 feet), Mount Blackburn (16,390 feet), and Mount Wrangell (14,163 feet). Blackburn, whose main outpourings of lava occurred some four million years ago, is now considered dead, while Sanford and Drum, whose eruptions continued into the past half-million years, are just sleeping. Wrangell, whose steam plume is

▼ *An aerial view of the western part of Mount Wrangell's ice-filled, three-by four-mile-wide caldera shows one area of steaming fumaroles on the rim. Although reports of ash explosions in the early 1900s are uncertain, a black and white photo of dark deposits (apparently volcanic ash) on the snow-covered summit was published by the U.S. Geological Survey in 1903.*

R. Motyka, Alaska Division of Geological and Geophysical Surveys

sometimes still visible on clear days, and whose small, reworked ash eruptions occasionally blacken its snow and ice-covered summit, is the live volcano of this great park.

Mount Wrangell is a large, ice-covered shield volcano with a 2.5 by 3.5-mile-wide summit caldera. It has often been climbed by experienced mountaineers, but it is easier to reach the summit by landing a ski-plane on its flat ice-filled caldera. There are three small craters with active fumaroles along the rim of the caldera. Baron von Wrangell, from whom the volcano takes its modern name, was Governor of Russian America during the 1830s. Its Indian name, K'elt'aeni, means "the one who controls the weather."

Most of Mount Wrangell was built by large, gently-sloping andesite flows from about 600,000 to 200,000 years ago, and the summit caldera possibly collapsed 50,000 years ago. At roughly that same time a large andesite flow from the summit area traveled more than 40 miles southwest into the Copper River Basin. Mount Zanetti, a large cinder cone on the northwest flank of Mount Wrangell, may have erupted less than 25,000 years ago. The small ash eruptions that typify historical activity apparently have not involved any new magma; instead they were probably steam explosions that expelled old rock fragments.

◄ **Opposite:**
Hooking a salmon in a tributary of the Copper River, a fisherman enjoys one of the most popular alternatives to volcano-watching in this vast park.

▼ **Below:**
The mining settlement of Kennecott was named for the Kennicott Glacier, apparently by someone who had trouble spelling. From the first shipment of high grade copper ore in 1911 to the final shipment in 1938, approximately $200 million worth of copper traveled 196 miles by railroad to the port of Cordova. Abandoned today, the mining town at its peak employed about 600 people.

Don Pitcher

▲ *Far from stores and conveniences, camping in this wilderness-oriented park appeals to hardy, self-sufficient visitors. A handful of lodges and bed-and-breakfast houses do exist, however.*

Ice and snow cover 90 percent of Mount Wrangell, feeding the many mountain glaciers that descend its flanks. Nabesna Glacier begins high on the southeast side of the volcano and flows more than fifty miles east, then north, where it melts to create the Nabesna River.

The calderas in the Wrangell volcanoes appear to have formed by withdrawal of magma and collapse, like Hawaiian calderas, rather than by explosion and collapse, like Aniakchak and Crater Lake calderas. However, there is at least one major and recent exception to this. Although geographically part of the St. Elias Mountains, Mount Churchill (15,638 feet) is geologically part of the Wrangell volcanic field.

Radiocarbon dating of widespread volcanic ash beds that lie on or near the surface of large areas in Eastern Alaska and the Yukon Territory of Canada point to two major explosive eruptions of Mount Churchill, one 1,900 years ago, the other 1,250 years ago. Together the ash layers from these two explosions cover 130,000 square miles and have a total volume of at least 12 cubic miles. Known as the White River Ash, this light gray layer, an inch to a foot or more in thickness, is exposed in many road cuts along the Alaska Highway between Tok, Alaska, and Whitehorse, Yukon Territory. The White River, named for its light muddy color, probably gets that mud from both rock-flour ground up by glaciers in the St. Elias Range and from erosion of the volcanic ash layer.

The thickness and distribution of the White River Ash clearly point to a small, now ice-filled caldera on the summit of Mount Churchill as its source. Without the outcrops of volcanic ash layers, the evidence for two of the largest explosive eruptions in North America during the past 2,000 years would be lost. These young, major explosive eruptions from the older part of a volcanic field considered to be mainly non-violent provide a sobering lesson: Surprise eruptions of great violence have happened well within the history of human habitation in this area, and they probably will again.

There is much to see and do for others besides volcanophiles in Wrangell-St. Elias National Park. Wilderness mountaineering, exploring mining ghost towns, fishing for trout and salmon, bird and game watching, river rafting, and kayaking in icy bays, to name a few. The Copper River and Malaspina areas are major flyways of migratory birds, including trumpeter swans. Dall sheep roam the rocky ridges, caribou, moose and bear—both black and grizzly—forage in the lower areas, and wildflowers bloom profusely in the long days of summer.

▼ *Wildlife abounds in the park's vast backcountry, including moose, Dall sheep and breath-taking flocks of nesting and migratory birds. Pictured below are the footprints of an Alaskan brown bear and a migratory Caribou.*

The summit of 18,008-foot Mount St. Elias is only 12 miles away from tidewater in Icy Bay. The Malaspina Glacier, larger than the state of Rhode Island, spreads out a fan of ice between the peaks and the sea. Again, we think the way to see these marvels is by light plane.

By automobile, Wrangell-St. Elias National Park can be reached by highways from Anchorage, from Valdez, and from Tok on the Alaska Highway. Park Headquarters is near Copper Center on the park's western boundary. However you decide to see the Wrangell volcanoes—by plane, by car, on skis, or on foot—we think that once there you will become a loyal subject of this "mountain kingdom."

Don Pitcher

National Park Service

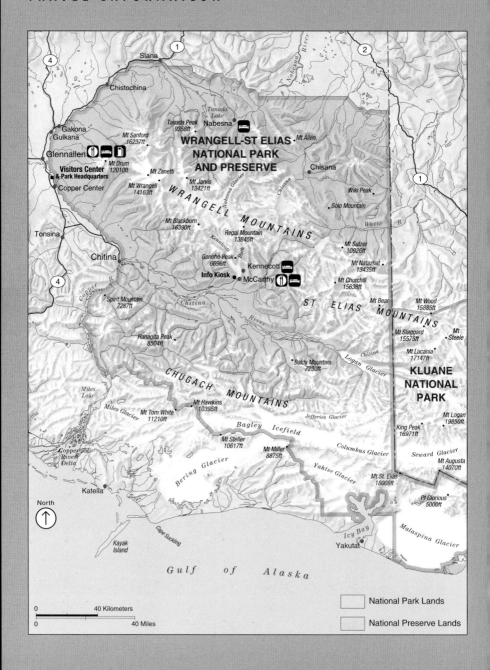

North

National Park Lands

National Preserve Lands

0   40 Kilometers

0   40 Miles

WRANGELL-ST. ELIAS
NATIONAL PARK AND PRESERVE

▶ **GETTING THERE**

Wrangell-St. Elias National Park is in southern Alaska, about 200 miles east of Anchorage. Two unpaved roads lead into the park: the Nabesna Road north of the Wrangell Mountains, and the Chitina/McCarthy Road, which reaches close to the old Kennecott copper mining town south of the Wrangells. The best way to see Mt. Wrangell and the other spectacular scenery in this huge area is to wait for good weather and hire a light plane. There is a major international airport in Anchorage.

▶ **ESSENTIALS**

There are no official facilities inside the park, but there are private lodges and bed & breakfast places on the McCarthy and Nabesna roads, and in McCarthy and Kennicott. The Visitor Center, open daily in summer and weekdays in winter, is near Copper Center on the Old Richardson Highway (milepost 101.5) just west of the preserve boundary. There are no fees.

▶ **CLIMATE**

Summer is generally cloudy and cool with some warm clear days. Early fall is often clear. Winter is cold and dark with temperature dropping to -50°F. Even in summer the weather can change very rapidly.

▶ **INFORMATION**

Wrangell-St. Elias National Park and Preserve
Post Office Box 439
Copper Center, AK 99573
Telephone: 907-822-5234
Website: www.nps.gov/wrst

▶ **VOLCANO FACTS**

Name – Mount Wrangell
Volcano type – shield volcano with caldera
Rock type – andesite
Height – 14,163 feet
Latest eruption – early 1900s

National Park Service

Part Three

VOLCANOES ASLEEP

Sleeping volcanoes are beautiful but dangerous; apparently the longer a volcano lies dormant, the more energy it stores up for some future eruption. Can geologists tell if a volcano is just sleeping and not dead? Since the final answer to that question lies in the future, there is no absolute "yes," but evidence from a volcano's past eruptions, and vital signs such as earthquakes, gas vents and hot springs, makes the practical answer "probably." If a particular volcano has had a life span of a million years, and its geologic past indicates that it has had previous periods of sleep of 200,000 years, then a record of no eruptions during the last 100,000 years is not a reliable indication of death. This is particularly true if some vital signs still exist.

In this section we discuss 13 volcanic areas that have erupted one or more times during the past 100,000 years, but did not erupt in the 20th century: One in Hawaii, one in Washington, two in Oregon, four in California, one in Idaho, one in Wyoming, two in New Mexico, and one in Arizona. Although the last eruption in Yellowstone National Park occurred 70,000 years ago, the large and vigorous geysers and hot springs, and occasional earthquake swarms are ample evidence that Yellowstone is sleeping, not dead.

> **Below:** *Riverside Geyser in Yellowstone National Park erupts to a maximum height of 75 feet every 5 1/2 to 8 1/2 hours.*
> **Opposite:** *The beautiful sleeping volcano, Mount Rainier, dominates the view from most parts of the national park.*

HALEAKALA
NATIONAL PARK, HAWAII

Almost all volcanic mountains are visually stunning, but the sight of an arrestingly beautiful volcano that rises more than 10,000 feet from the blue Hawaiian ocean is truly unforgettable. Haleakala, the youngest volcano on the island of Maui, soars to 10,023 feet above its 33-mile diameter base. But that's only part of the story; more than 90 percent of the mass of the mountain is submarine. Measured from its much wider base on the ocean floor, its elevation would be 28,000 feet.

Haleakala volcano was born at the Hawaiian Hot Spot, which we've described on pages 15-17. After growing quietly underwater for many thousands of years it emerged from the sea about a million years ago, to take its place in the Hawaiian chain as a neighbor to the older and larger West Maui volcano. By 750,000 years ago, Haleakala had grown to become the main volcano of the Hawaiian Hot Spot.

Over many thousands of years Haleakala grew to a height that geologists say probably reached 13,000 to 14,000 feet, with its summit about a mile or so east of the current high spot, Pu'u Ula Ula, or Red Hill.

What could account for the loss of several thousand feet of elevation? Three factors were at work: First, Hawaiian volcanoes gradually sink because their great weight slowly bends the Earth's crust downward beneath them. Sinking even a small fraction of an inch per year adds up over a half-million years. Second, the summits of shield volcanoes in their mature stage are apt to collapse into huge basins or craters, called calderas. Third, and the easiest to find evidence for, is the powerful force of erosion. About 300,000 years ago Haleakala's volcanic activity slowed, and at the same time a period of torrential rains set in. Streams that flowed down what are now called Kaupo and Keanae valleys swelled into raging rivers. They deepened and

▼ *Trails in Haleakala Crater wind among these colorful, geologically-young cinder cones. Radiocarbon dates indicate that they are between 800 and 4,000 years old.*

John Kjargaard

lengthened the valleys until the streamheads almost met at the summit, scouring out or at least deepening the vast crater and cutting deeply into older lava flows.

Then about 20,000 years ago, in another of Earth's endless cycles, volcanic activity renewed, with lava partly filling the vast crater and flowing down the stream-cut valleys. The colorful cinder cones and crater-floor flows that you see today are all products of this later volcanism. It's a complicated history, and geologists are still trying to date Haleakala's many lava flows to find more pieces of the puzzle.

What of Haleakala's future? Though it is sliding slowly away from the Hawaiian hot spot and the volcanic fireworks have moved to the Big Island of Hawaii, Haleakala is considered to be only dormant and will probably still awaken for a last fling or two. No one is certain when Haleakala last erupted, but Hawaiian oral history seems to place it at about 1790. There is some interesting evidence to confirm that time period. Two European explorers, the Count de La Perouse in 1786 and George Vancouver in 1793, each made a careful chart of Maui's southwest coast. The chart made by La Perouse shows a broad, shallow bay between two headlands, but on Vancouver's later chart there is a distinct peninsula in the bay, which must have formed when lava flowed into the sea.

▲ **Above:** The sweeping view across Haleakala Crater has often been called a "moonscape," but the interplay of light, shadow, and color makes it more fascinating than stark.

▼ **Below:** The Hawaiian name for the luminous silversword plant is ahinahina, the word for "moonlight," repeated.

▲ *Above: Clouds creep over the crater rim of Haleakala.*

▼ *Below: Close-up of the intricate pattern of an unfolding fern frond.*

That story, though appealing, may not be the last word. New radiocarbon dates on samples of charcoal taken from beneath the flow indicate the eruption that produced it probably occurred sometime between AD 1480 and 1600. Whichever date turns out to be correct, Haleakala is definitely only sleeping.

As volcanoes go, Haleakala is an easy one to visit since a good road goes all the way to the summit. If you only have one day to spend at the park, just the drive itself, from sea level to 10,000 feet, is a grand experience. But when you reach the crater rim, the view that unfolds before you is breathtaking. It has often been called a "moonscape"; if so, it's a moonscape in Technicolor, with multihued cinder cones, jumbled lava flows and stark cliffs. The views are ever-changing as shadows and clouds shift.

Four viewpoints—Leleiwi, Kalahaku, Haleakala Visitor Center, and Pu'u Ula Ula—afford grand views of the immense Haleakala Crater, which measures 7.5 miles long east to west, 2.5 miles wide, and 3,000 feet deep. These views are from different perspectives and altitudes, but are equally breathtaking. Sunsets seen from Haleakala's summit are wonderful, but the favorite seems to be the incomparable spectacle of the sun rising over the crater's rim.

Glen Kaye, NPS

National Park Service

▲ **Above:** *Hikers brave the Halemau'u Trail, which descends 2,000 feet into Haleakala Crater.*

▼ **Below:** *Ohi'a Lehua.*

Dawn comes early to the summit of Haleakala, but every morning a crowd of shivering sunrise-watchers gather at the Pu'u Ula Ula overlook to see the first rays of the sun break over the crater rim and a sea of dawn-red clouds. It is a new show every day; as shadows retreat from the dark recesses, the giant crater comes alive with color, and its strange and unearthly shapes are revealed.

Haleakala National Park extends from the far rim of the crater down to the sea. It is possible to hike on trails across the crater and down to the coastal road through the Kaupo Gap, but it's a two-day hike and you will need to arrange a pickup by car at Kaupo.

Kipahulu Valley descends from the east rim of the Crater to the ocean through a dense tropical rainforest. The scenery in the lower part of this valley, known simply as Kipahulu, is totally different from that at the summit; instead of barren lava flows and cinder cones, it is marked by lush, almost impenetrable foliage and deep canyons with cascading streams and pools. There is no direct connection inside the park by road. To reach Kipahulu, drive back to the coast and follow State Highway 360, the infamous Hana Highway, with its hairpin curves, 56 narrow bridges, and incomparable tropical scenery.

John Kjargaard

From the Kipahulu Ranger Station, trails lead to an ancient Hawaiian village and up the canyon to a spectacular waterfall. Upper Kipahulu Valley, though, has been designated a Biological Reserve, and is open only to scientists for research. This remote valley is a haven for many of Hawaii's endangered species of plants and birds, most of which live nowhere else on Earth.

The name Haleakala means "House of the Sun," and the sun has always figured prominently in Hawaiian mythology, as in the story of the demigod Maui's greatest feat. Legend says that long ago the days were short with only three or four hours of daylight, because the sun was so lazy he wanted to hurry across the sky to get home to bed. Maui's mother was a maker of fine tapa fabric that needed long hours of sunlight to dry properly, so she went to her son for help. Maui had noticed that the sun rose over Haleakala by snaking one long beam and then another over the crater's rim, in the same way a spider climbs onto a ledge. One night Maui took a sack of strong snares he had woven from vines, and hid in a cave near the summit. As each of the sun's legs appeared over the rim he threw a snare around it and tied them fast to a *wiliwili* tree. The sun pleaded to be set free, but was in no position to bargain. He had to agree to Maui's demand that he walk slowly and steadily across the sky, as he has done to this day.

▲ **Above:** *The bloom stalk of the silversword or ahi - nahina, a plant unique to Maui. They live from a few to 50 years, bloom once, and then die.*

▼ **Bottom:** *Sunrise over cloud-filled Haleakala Crater provides one of the most popular views in the park.*

Roger Henneberger

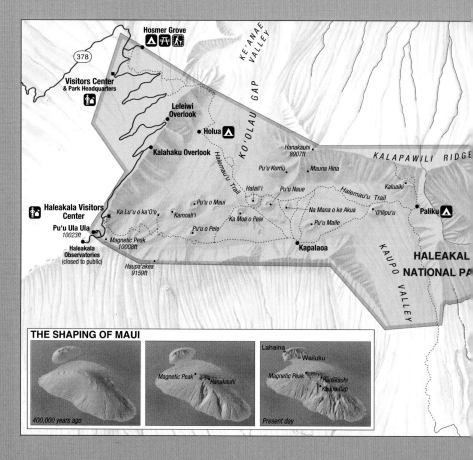

378

Hosmer Grove

Visitors Center
& Park Headquarters

Leleiwi Overlook

Holua

Kalahaku Overlook

KE'ANAE VALLEY

KO'OLAU GAP

Hanakauhi 8907ft

Pu'u Kumu

Mauna Hina

KALAPAWILI RIDGE

Halali'i

Pu'u Naue

Kaluaiki

Halemau'u Trail

Halemau'u Trail

Haleakala Visitors Center

Ka Lu'u o ka'O'o

Pu'u o Maui

Kamoali'i

Na Mana o ke Akua

O'ilipu'u

Paliku

Pu'u Ula Ula
10023ft

Ka Moa o Pele

Pu'u Maile

Haleakala Observatories
(closed to public)

Magnetic Peak 10008ft

Pu'u o Pele

Kapalaoa

KAUPO VALLEY

**HALEAKAL
NATIONAL PA**

Haupa'akea 9159ft

THE SHAPING OF MAUI

400,000 years ago

Magnetic Peak

Hanakauhi

Lahaina
Wailuku

Magnetic Peak

Hanakauhi
Kaupo Gap

Present day

Pincushion protea grow on flower farms outside the park on the way up the Summit Road.

▶ GETTING THERE

Haleakala National Park is located on the Hawaiian island of Maui, served by frequent flights to Kahului Airport. State highways 37, 377, and 378 lead 36 miles to the summit (follow the signs). The remote Kipahulu Visitor Center on the southeast coast is reached by State Highway 360, the long and winding Hana Highway.

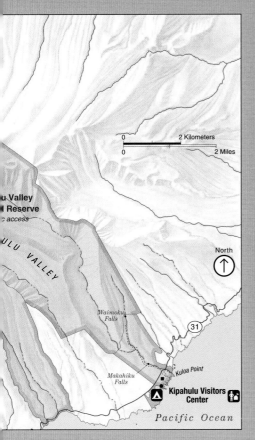

u Valley
Reserve
c access

ULU VALLEY

Waimoku
Falls

31

North
↑

Makahiku
Falls

Kuloa Point

Kipahulu Visitors
Center

Pacific Ocean

▶ **CLIMATE**

Tropical temperatures at sea level cool about 3°F. for every 1,000 feet of increased elevation. Daytime temperatures at the summit range from about 40° to 65°F. and sometimes reach below freezing at night. Fog and rain are possible.

▶ **INFORMATION**

Haleakala National Park
Post Office Box 369
Makawao, HI 96768
Telephone: 808-572-4400
Website: www.nps.gov/hale

▶ **VOLCANO FACTS**

Name – Haleakala
Type of volcano – shield volcano
Rock type – basalt
Height – 10,023 feet
Oldest rocks – about 1,000,000 years
Latest eruption – 1790?

Ama'uma'u fern.

▶ **ESSENTIALS**

Entrance fees are collected year round. The park is open 24 hours per day. There is no lodging, food, or gasoline available in the park, but there is a campground at Hosmer Grove. There are three visitor centers: the Park Headquarters Visitor Center on State Highway 378 as you enter the park; the Haleakala Visitor Center at the summit; and the Kipahulu Visitor Center on the coastal section of the park.

MOUNT RAINIER
NATIONAL PARK, WASHINGTON

It would be hard to imagine a more magnificently impressive mountain than Washington's Mount Rainier. At 14,411 feet in altitude, it soars above the countryside in splendid isolation, with no high mountains nearby for contrast. Its gleaming icy summit is covered with more than 25 glaciers that stream down its sides to meet subalpine meadows lush with summer wildflowers, which give way in turn at timberline to dense forests of giant conifers. Add to this the icy glacial streams and waterfalls, clear lakes and many miles of hiking trails, and you have one of our finest national parks.

The allure of Mount Rainier rests not just on its majestic size and elusive beauty, but includes an air of mystery and more than a hint of danger. It is, after all, an active volcano, and even a small eruption would disrupt the lives of the 2.5 million people living in Mount Rainier's shadow, in ways ranging from inconvenient to disastrous.

Mount Rainier is the tallest of the fifteen great volcanoes that make up the backbone of the Cascade Range, from Lassen Peak in California to Mount Garibaldi in British Columbia, and that range is part of the thousand-volcano Ring of Fire that surrounds the Pacific Ocean. Most Cascade volcanoes are stratovolcanoes, built of a combination of hard lava flows alternating with layers of ash and fragmental debris from explosive eruptions. Mount Rainier is a good example of this type of volcano. Evidence shows that over its long history it has produced thousands of lava flows, some of enormous size, as well as thousands of explosive ash eruptions. Geologists trying to understand the volcano's life story study the many layers of lava, ash, and pumice deposits, as well as deposits left by massive mudflows.

◄ **Opposite:** Famed for some of the most spectacular wildflower displays on the continent, Mount Rainier (seen here from Paradise Meadows) is an outdoor textbook for botanists. The dark rock bulging from the right side of Mount Rainier's profile is Gibraltar Rock, a familiar landmark to climbers since one of the summit routes passes close to it.

▼ **Below:** Fields of avalanche lilies burst into bloom as they follow the retreating snowfields up Mount Rainier's meadows.

▲ **Above:** *There are twenty-five major glaciers on 14,411-foot-high Mount Rainier, though only a few are visible in this picture. Counted together, they contain one cubic mile of ice.*

▼ **Below:** *The Nisqually Glacier carved this U-shaped valley, but it has retreated more than a mile since 1830, and its snout is just out of sight in this photo. The ice was much thicker also, as shown by the scars on the valley walls.*

▶ **Opposite:** *Fall colors at Paradise warn that more winter snow will soon feed Rainier's many glaciers. Only a few small steam vents remind climbers to the summit that this volcano is not dead, only sleeping.*

▲ *Sunbeam Creek cascades down from a small glacier at the north base of The Castle and Pinnacle Peak in the Tatoosh Range, where rock climbers gather to hone their skills on the steep cliffs.*

But Mount Rainier is also a classic example of the battle of opposing natural forces: built by fire and torn by ice. It is hard to decipher all the details of the mountain's past since so much has been ground away by the relentlessly moving rivers of ice. Recent studies place its age at about a half-million years— young by geologic standards—with its latest eruption about 150 years ago. Most volcanologists agree that that was only its latest, not its last, eruption. Mount Rainier seems to be sleeping peacefully now, but some time in the future it will almost surely stir to life again. As of now no one can predict when the next activity will be, or of what nature.

The same features that make Mount Rainier so arrestingly beautiful—its height, steepness and its massive cap of snow and ice—also make it potentially very dangerous. Even a modest sized eruption of hot lava and rock debris would melt glacier ice and snow, sending huge mud and debris flows racing down the mountainside. Some prehistoric flows reached as far as 100 miles.

One of Mount Rainier's most destructive eruptions occurred about 5,600 years ago, when a catastrophic collapse of the whole summit of the mountain—a volume estimated at one cubic mile—sent the enormous Osceola mudflow roaring down the White River Valley to Puget Sound. Small and large towns are now clustered on top of that ancient mudflow deposit.

On a clear day, Mount Rainier so dominates the landscape that even from a hundred miles away you are conscious of its looming presence. Driving closer, you begin to comprehend its overwhelming size.

For closer views of Mount Rainier and its glaciers, Paradise Park is the place to start. A modern visitor center tells the mountain's story, and points the way to the many miles of trails winding through flowery meadows. One trail leads to a viewpoint overlooking the Nisqually Glacier for an unforgettable

▲ **Above:** *Columbia lily.*

▼ **Below:** *This roadside view of Mount Rainier beyond Tipsoo Lake is one of the best in the park. Tipsoo means "grassy lake" in Chinook jargon–a mixture of Native American, English, and French languages.*

look at the slow-moving ice. Others lead uphill from the visitor center for a close encounter with the permanent ice fields. A day spent wandering the many miles of trails at Paradise will convince you that the name is fitting.

Most summit climbs start from Paradise and entail an arduous two-day trip for experienced climbers. Unless you are an expert climber, don't try a summit attempt without a guide. From the early 19th century, when emigrants were heading west, the thought of standing atop this towering mountain has proved irresistible to a surprising number of people. The first well documented climb was in 1852. Today, as many as 5,000 people actually reach the summit every year, though more that twice that number attempt it. Some are dedicated climbers, but more than a few modern-day emigrants—Seattle's cyber-millionaires—have been lured from their computers long enough to make the trek to Mount Rainier's summit.

◄ Opposite: Crevasses make climbing on Mount Rainier's snowfields and glaciers both difficult and dangerous.

▲ Above: The summit of Mount Rainier, known as Columbia Crest, Little Tahoma (the sharp peak on the left), and Liberty Cap (on the right), are all visible from the visitor center at Sunrise.

National Park Service

▶ At right: Elk are frequent visitors to Mount Rainier's meadows.

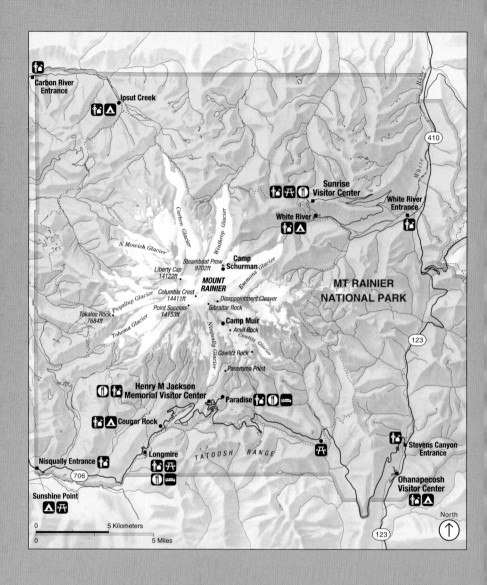

Carbon River
Entrance

Ipsut Creek

Sunrise
Visitor Center

White River
Entrance

White River

MT RAINIER
NATIONAL PARK

Carbon Glacier

Windthrop Glacier

N Mowich Glacier

Steamboat Prow
9702ft

Camp
Schurman

Emmons Glacier

Liberty Cap
14122ft

MOUNT
RAINIER

Columbia Crest
14411ft

Disappointment Cleaver

Gibraltar Rock

Puyallup Glacier

Point Success
14153ft

Tokaloo Rock
7684ft

Tahoma Glacier

Camp Muir

Anvil Rock

Nisqually Glacier

Cowlitz Glacier

Cowlitz Rock

Panorama Point

Henry M Jackson
Memorial Visitor Center

Paradise

Cougar Rock

Stevens Canyon
Entrance

Nisqually Entrance

Longmire

TATOOSH   RANGE

Ohanapecosh
Visitor Center

706

Sunshine Point

410

123

123

0   5 Kilometers

0   5 Miles

North

142

MOUNT RAINIER NATIONAL PARK

▶**GETTING THERE**

Located in west-central Washington, about a two-hour drive from Seattle, Mount Ranier lies close to the Seattle-Tacoma International Airport (65 miles) and Oregon's Portland International Airport (150 miles). Six different roads enter the park from all four compass directions, but State Highways 706, 123, and 410 provide the principle routes for motorists.

▶**ESSENTIALS**

Entrance fees are collected year-round. The Longmire Museum is open year-round. Visitor centers at Ohanapecosh and Sunrise are open June to October. The Henry M. Jackson Memorial Visitor Center at Paradise is open daily from mid-April to October, and on weekends and holidays in October through April. There are two hotels in Mount Rainier National Park--the National Park Inn at Longmire (open all year) and the historic Paradise Inn at Paradise (open mid-May to early October). Both are operated by Mount Rainier Guest Services (for reservations call 360-569-2275). Several campgrounds are also available in the park. Meals are served at National Park Inn and Paradise Inn; snacks are available at the Jackson Memorial Visitor Center and Sunrise Lodge. Picnic supplies are available at National Park Inn General Store and at Sunrise Lodge. There are no gas stations in the park.

▶**CLIMATE**

From mid-June through August the weather is usually mild and sunny, though a rain shower is not unusual. Late spring and fall are usually very rainy, and winter snowfall is heavy.

▶**INFORMATION**

Mount Rainier National Park
Tahoma Woods, Star Route
Ashford, WA 98304-9751
Telephone: 360-569-2211
Web site: www.nps.gov/mora/

▶**VOLCANO FACTS**

Name – Mount Rainier
Volcano type – stratovolcano
Rock type – andesite
Height – 14,411 feet
Oldest dated rocks – 500,000 years
Latest eruption – between 1820 and 1854

Avalanche lily

CRATER LAKE
NATIONAL PARK, OREGON

NPS

Sapphire-blue Crater Lake, encircled by cliffs, is one of the most beautiful places on Earth. One element of its great beauty is surprise. The approaches to the lake climb through towering trees, flower filled meadows, and clear mountain air. Then suddenly, on reaching the rim of the crater, the view of this magnificent, nearly circular lake—six miles across and 1,000 feet below your overlook—is a thought-stopper. Most first-time viewers can just say "Wow."

Rim Drive is a 33-mile road that circles Crater Lake. The road stays close to the rim, offering many spectacular views of the lake and the cliffs that surround it. The sunlight changes intensity and direction while you circle the rim, so the color and reflections from the lake also change. The intense blue of the lake results from the absorption of red and yellow colors in sunlight, and the scattering of blue light by the clear lake water.

The story of Crater Lake begins half a million years ago when a vigorous young volcano was born. Eruptions of andesitic ash and lava every few decades or centuries slowly built a great stratovolcano over this part of the Cascade subduction zone. Major earthquakes occasionally shook the region, and mountain glaciers gouged deep valleys on the volcano's high flanks.

By 8,000 years ago, after the last ice age, the great volcano, now named Mount Mazama, had grown to a height near 12,000 feet, but major changes were about to occur. Explosions blasted out a crater on the north side of Mazama, and a rhyodacite lava dome, now named Llao Rock, squeezed up to fill the crater. Rhyodacite is a volcanic rock midway in composition between dacite and rhyolite. Some 100 years later, approximately 5700 BC, the huge caldera-forming eruption began. No one knows how long it lasted, but evidence from other caldera eruptions, particularly that of Krakatau in Indonesia in 1883, suggests these great eruptions may build up slowly over months and then culminate in a giant outburst and collapse that lasts only hours to days.

▲ *Above:* *Devil's Backbone, a rock formation in the wall of Crater Lake, is a dark, vertical dike. A dike is a magma-filled fracture–now hardened and exposed–that was injected into the ancient volcano.*

▶ *Opposite:* *Pinnacles of rock eroded into strange hoodoo shapes outcrop on the walls of several canyons around Crater Lake. As ash flows from the huge eruption cooled, steam escaped upward along vertical fractures forming thousands of fuming gas vents. During the many years it took to cool the hot avalanche deposits, these rising vapors cemented the pumice and ash into more solid rock. Erosion, wind and gravity has etched out these once-underground steam pipes into steep pinnacles.*

▼ *Below:* *Western pasque flowers.*

The great outburst at Mount Mazama spewed out 12 cubic miles of rhyodacite magma, mostly in enormous glowing avalanches of hot ash and pumice fragments that swept down all sides of the mountain at race-car speeds. By volume, the eruption was 100 times larger than the 1980 eruption of Mount St. Helens, and 10 times larger than that of Krakatau. The pyroclastic flows reached as far as 30 miles from the summit and created the great apron of volcanic deposits that surround the mountain. All life was snuffed out beneath this thick, deadly blanket. Volcanic ash particles hurled high into the stratosphere fell like gray snow over a much larger area, even as far away as Canada.

Beneath this volcanic maelstrom, the great caldera was collapsing into the void from which the magma was erupting. Earthquakes must have been nearly continuous, and the legendary battle of the gods was in full sway. Finally the eruption was spent, and the black cloud that had jetted as high as 30 miles above the volcano slowly settled and cleared. Days of darkness became light again, and the vast steaming pit that had once been Mount Mazama was revealed. Cliffs up to 3,000 feet high encircled the barren caldera, and rockfalls tumbled into the newborn inferno.

Over many decades the huge caldera was slowly filled by rain and melting snow. Grass and flowers and forests began to clothe the thick blanket of barren debris on its outer flanks. Over centuries, nature has replaced the great violence and chaos with great beauty.

Several eruptions have occurred since the huge collapse. A small volcano within the caldera, Merriam Cone, is hidden underwater on the north side of Crater Lake. Wizard Island, the cinder cone that rises above the lake surface, largely grew about 300 years after the caldera formed. The youngest dated rocks come from a small underwater lava dome that erupted about 5,000 years ago. Will Mazama erupt again? We say "yes." When? Probably not in your lifetime.

Crater Lake is more than 1,900 feet deep, the deepest lake in the United States. Its clarity is remarkable; visibility through the water exceeds 140 feet, and a small amount of surface light dimly reaches the bottom. Scientists descending to the lake floor in a small submarine in 1989 discovered warm springs and fluffy yellow mats of bacteria fed by these mineral waters. These are vital signs that Mount Mazama is only sleeping.

◀ Opposite: This spectacular 1,200-foot-high cliff known as Llao Rock is part of the wall encircling Crater Lake. By studying the lava and ash layers in the walls from base to top, geologists have been able to decipher much of the long history of the growth of Mount Mazama, its great eruption, and its ultimate collapse.

▼ Below:A winter photo from the air clearly shows the almost circular, five-mile wide lake. Yearly snowfall at Crater Lake can total as much as 50 feet, but the record snowpack at any one time is 21 feet.

National Park Service

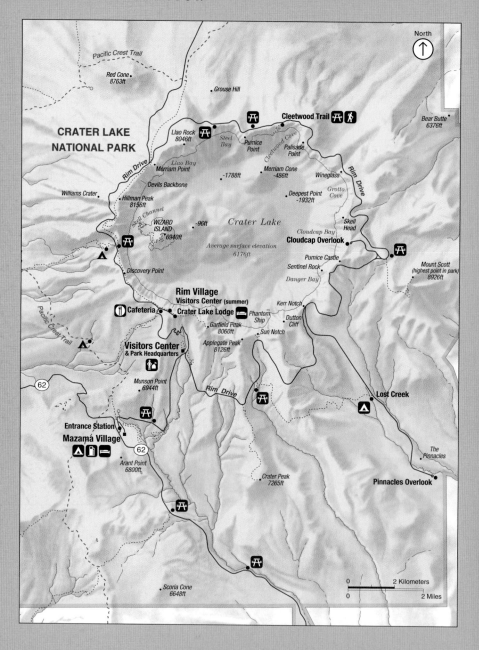

North

CRATER LAKE
NATIONAL PARK

Pacific Crest Trail

Red Cone
8763ft

Grouse Hill

Bear Butte
6376ft

Cleetwood Trail

Llao Rock
8046ft

Steel
Bay

Pumice
Point

Palisade
Point

Rim Drive

Merriam Point

Llao Bay

Devils Backbone

-1788ft

Merriam Cone
-486ft

Wineglass

Williams Crater

Hillman Peak
8156ft

Skell Channel

Deepest Point
-1932ft

Grotto
Cove

Rim Drive

WIZARD
ISLAND
6940ft

-96ft

Crater Lake

Skell
Head

Cloudcap Bay

Cloudcap Overlook

Mount Scott
(highest point in park)
8926ft

Average surface elevation
6176ft

Pumice Castle

Discovery Point

Sentinel Rock

Danger Bay

Rim Village
Visitors Center (summer)

Cafeteria

Crater Lake Lodge

Kerr Notch

Phantom
Ship

Pacific Crest Trail

Garfield Peak
8060ft

Dutton
Cliff

Sun Notch

Visitors Center
& Park Headquarters

Applegate Peak
8126ft

Munson Point
6944ft

Rim Drive

62

Lost Creek

Entrance Station

Mazama Village

62

Arant Point
6800ft

The
Pinnacles

Crater Peak
7265ft

Pinnacles Overlook

0   2 Kilometers

0   2 Miles

Scoria Cone
6648ft

CRATER LAKE NATIONAL PARK

▶ **GETTING THERE**

Crater Lake National Park is located in south-central Oregon. The west and south entrances on State Highway 62 are open all year. The north entrance off State Highway 138 is open July to September. The closest airports are in Medford, Oregon, 80 miles away, and Klamath Falls, Oregon, 54 miles away.

▶ **CLIMATE**

Generally dry and sunny weather prevails July through early September, with some afternoon thunderstorms. Summer temperatures average 70°F. during days and 40°F. at night. Snow, possible any time of year, falls heavy in winter, providing snowshoeing and cross-country skiing.

▶ **ESSENTIALS**

Food service, groceries, picnic areas, and gasoline are available from mid-June through early October. Limited food service and ski shop are available in winter. There are campgrounds, and seasonal lodging is available at Crater Lake Lodge (541-594-2511). Entrance fees are collected from June through September or later, if weather permits. There are two visitor centers, one at the Caldera Rim Village, and one at Park Headquarters.

▶ **INFORMATION**

Crater Lake National Park
Post Office Box 7
Crater Lake, OR 97604
Telephone: 541-594-2211
Website: www.nps.gov/crla

▶ **VOLCANO FACTS**

Name – Mount Mazama
Volcano type – caldera
Rock types – andesite to rhyodacite
Height – before collapse 7,700 years ago
    about 12,000 feet; presently 8,156 feet
Volume of caldera forming eruption –
    12 cubic miles of magma
Oldest dated rocks – 400,000 years
Youngest dated rocks – 5,000 years,
    from lava dome beneath the lake

Clarks nutcracker

K. Bacher, NPS

NEWBERRY
NATIONAL VOLCANIC MONUMENT, OREGON

Relatively unknown compared to Crater Lake, its neighbor only 70 miles to the southwest, Newberry Volcano is a hidden gem. Although its summit is less than 8,000 feet high, Newberry's volume makes it the largest young volcano in the 48 adjacent states. Its summit caldera contains two beautiful lakes and a thick obsidian flow only 1,300 years old. On the flanks of the sleeping volcano there are lava tubes, a "lava-cast forest," and hundreds of cinder cones, including one with a road to the top. As if this is not enough, there are hot springs within the caldera lakes and three major waterfalls nearby. Besides these geologic wonders, the monument provides roads and trails through beautiful conifer forests and wildflower meadows, as well as superb fishing in the lakes and streams.

Newberry is a shield volcano about 30 miles long, north to south, and 20 miles wide, east to west. The highest point on the southeast rim of the summit caldera, Paulina Peak (7,984 feet), rises some 4,000 feet above the general elevation of the surrounding region. Lava flows extend more than 50 miles north of the caldera, beyond the Oregon cities of Bend and Redmond. This shield volcano is unusual in that it has erupted not only basalt, but andesite, dacite and rhyolite as well—more silica-rich lavas and pyroclastic deposits than are generally associated with stratovolcanoes.

The caldera, called Newberry Crater, is about 1,000 feet deep and spreads over an area about five miles long and four miles wide. It formed by the collapse of a once-higher volcano during several major eruptions that removed large volumes of magma from deep beneath its once 9,000- to 10,000-foot summit. The earliest of these great

▼ Newberry Crater–actually a caldera–is about 1,000 feet deep and four- to five-miles wide. It formed by collapse during several eruptions that occurred between 500,000 and 200,000 years ago. In this view from the air, East Lake is seen in the foreground, and the snow covered area beyond the lake is Big Obsidian Flow, only 1,300 years old.

Robert Jensen

eruptions apparently occurred as long as half a million years ago, and the latest about 200,000 years ago. Lava flows and pyroclastic deposits have been filling the caldera ever since, so its maximum depth was once much greater.

Beautiful Paulina Lake and East Lake nestle within the caldera. Once devoid of fish, these cold, clear lakes have been stocked with trout and salmon. The snow-melt water is generally frigid, but hot springs near the lake edges warm it up a bit. Geologic evidence indicates molten rock may still underlie the caldera at a depth of only two to three miles. Should you worry about that? No, hot springs don't heat up as fast as they did in the movie *Dante's Peak*.

The latest activity of Newberry Volcano was a major eruption about 1,300 years ago. It began with a high explosion column that showered pumice lumps and ashes over much of the east side of the

▲ *Three of the many cinder cones on the flank of the Newberry Volcano can be seen in this photo taken from Paulina Peak, the 7,984-foot summit of Newberry's caldera rim.*

▲ *Big Obsidian Flow (in the right foreground), a thick lava flow of viscous rhyolite more than one square mile in area, erupted on the floor of Newberry caldera 1,300 years ago. Obsidian is the raw material for making the sharp, glassy black arrow points used by many Native Americans. Thick layers of rhyolite ash surrounding and beneath the flow indicate that the beginning of the Big Obsidian eruption was highly explosive. Paulina Lake and East Lake can be seen beyond the flow.*

volcano. This was followed by a large pyroclastic flow that spewed from the same vent near the south caldera wall, racing down into Paulina Lake. The final episode of the eruption produced the Big Obsidian Flow, a thick rhyolite flow that covers more than a square mile. The relatively barren surface of the flow and the concentric ridges surrounding its vent make it the most prominent volcanic feature in the monument. Its "youth," only 1,300 years, makes it the youngest dated lava flow in Oregon.

Other rhyolite flows and pumice falls occurred about 3,500 years ago near East Lake. Around 7,000 years ago large volumes of basaltic lavas poured out of a northwest rift on the flank of the volcano, after a series of rhyolite eruptions occurred in the area between the lakes. The north flank eruptions created lava tubes, a "forest" of lava casts as a flow inundated an ancient pine forest, and many cinder cones, including Lava Butte. Where molten lava surrounds a tree trunk, the steam from the heated wood cools and hardens a layer of lava around the trunk. Later, as the wood burns out or rots away, it leaves a hole in the hardened flow—a mold of a long-gone tree.

Lava Butte, a cinder cone with a road to its 500-foot-high summit, is just east of US Highway 97, about 20 miles north of the caldera. It provides magnificent views of the Cascade peaks to the west. The visitor center near its base, called Lava Lands, is the best starting place for exploring Newberry Volcano. It has informative exhibits and detailed handouts on how to reach the many features in this volcanic wonderland. Those who like cave exploring, for instance, should ask directions to Lava River Cave, accessible by a short road about a mile south on US Highway 97. At one place Highway 97 crosses over the lava tube, 50 feet below. It's nature's subway; take two flashlights.

Newberry National Volcanic Monument is managed by the U.S. Forest Service, and forest roads provide access to many of the interesting and beautiful features at Newberry. A paved highway reaches Paulina and East Lake, and the edge of the Big Obsidian Flow. Climb the trail up the steep front of the flow to see tons of this black volcanic glass, a favorite raw material for the arrowheads and knives of American Indians.

Spending a day or two at Newberry offers a fantastic field education in volcanology. We know of no other place where you can easily visit and see so many volcanic features and rock types in one location. Will you see an eruption while you're there? Probably not. Will Newberry Volcano ever erupt again? Almost certainly yes.

▼ *The Crater Rim Trail encircles the caldera with a 21-mile loop that provides impressive views of volcanic hoodoos on the rim, and the lakes that partially fill the floor. The Paulina Lake Trail encircles the biggest lake with a much easier, and flatter, seven-mile loop.*

George Wuerthner

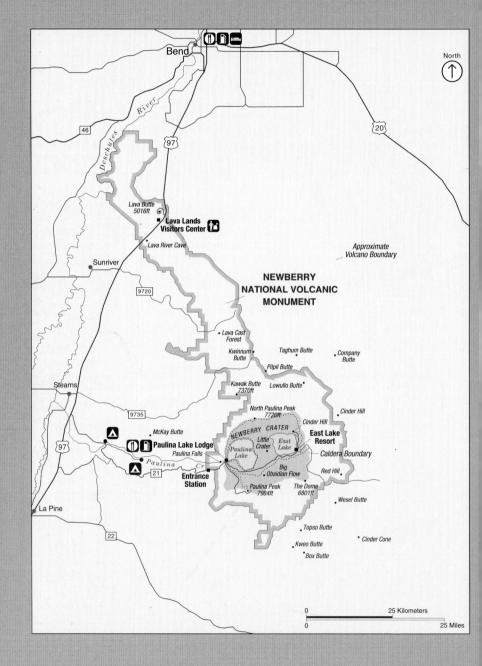

North

Bend

River

46

97

Deschutes

20

Lava Butte
5016ft

**Lava Lands
Visitors Center**

Lava River Cave

Sunriver

Approximate
Volcano Boundary

**NEWBERRY
NATIONAL VOLCANIC
MONUMENT**

9720

Lava Cast
Forest

Kwinnum
Butte

Taghum Butte

Company
Butte

Pilpil Butte

Stearns

Kawak Butte
7370ft

Lowullo Butte

9735

North Paulina Peak
7720ft

Cinder Hill

Cinder Hill

McKay Butte

NEWBERRY CRATER

East Lake
Resort

Paulina Lake Lodge

Paulina Falls

Little
Crater

East
Lake

Paulina
Lake

Caldera Boundary

97

Paulina

Cr

Big
Obsidian Flow

Red Hill

21

**Entrance
Station**

Paulina Peak
7984ft

The Dome
6801ft

Wesel Butte

La Pine

22

Topso Butte

Kweo Butte

Cinder Cone

Box Butte

0		25 Kilometers
0		25 Miles

NEWBERRY
NATIONAL VOLCANIC MONUMENT

Young marmots. NPS

▸ **GETTING THERE**

Newberry National Volcanic Monument is located south of Bend, in eastern, central Oregon. There is a commercial airport in Redmond, 25 miles north of Lava Lands Visitor Center on US Highway 97; the nearest large airport is in Portland, 160 miles from Bend. Forest Service Road 21 to Newberry Caldera turns east from US Highway 97, 25 miles south of Bend.

▸ **ESSENTIALS**

There are resorts on Paulina Lake (open all year; telephone 541-536-2240) and on East Lake (open in summer; telephone 541-536-2230). Both have general stores, food service, cabins, boat rentals, and gasoline. There are also several public campgrounds in the caldera, and public boat ramps. Ask about use permit fees at Lava Lands Visitor Center (541-593-2421), open late April to early October.

▸ **CLIMATE**

Dry and sunny during late June through September, with some afternoon thunderstorms. Summer temperatures are mild but cool at night. Cold and snow prevail in winter, when the monument is open for snowmobiling and cross-country skiing.

▸ **INFORMATION**

Newberry National Volcanic Monument
Deschutes National Forest
1645 Highway 20 East
Bend, OR 97701
Telephone: 541-383-5300
Website: www.fs.fed.us/r6/deschutes/monument/monument.html

▸ **VOLCANO FACTS**

Name – Newberry
Volcano type – shield volcano with caldera
Rock types – basalt to rhyolite
Height – before collapses about 9,000 to 10,000 feet; presently 7,984 feet
Oldest dated rocks – about 1.2 million years
Youngest dated rocks – 1,300 years (Big Obsidian Flow)

Newberry knotweed turns bright red after the first autumn frost.

159

LAVA BEDS
NATIONAL MONUMENT, CALIFORNIA

▼ **Below:** *Most of the lava flows and cinder cones in Lava Beds are basaltic, roughly similar in composition to Hawaiian lavas. The Mammoth Crater flow that issued from the Medicine Lake shield volcano about 30,000 years ago is the largest in the monument and it hosts most of the lava-tube caves in the area. The cinder cone in this photo has the typical 30° slopes that form as loose cinders pile up by fall-back around an erupting vent, and slide into their angle of repose.*

▶ **Opposite:** *Although softened by wildflowers, Devil's Homestead Lava Flow is typical of the park's rugged terrain that makes cross-country travel so difficult.*

Lava Beds National Monument, 72 square miles of lava flows on the north slope of Medicine Lake Volcano in Northern California, is famous both for its lava tube caves, and as the setting of the 1872-1873 Modoc Indian War.

Although the summit caldera of Medicine Lake Volcano is eight miles south of the monument, describing the volcano responsible for the lava beds is the logical place to begin. Gentle in slope compared to the striking 14,164-foot-high cone of Mount Shasta, 30 miles southwest, Medicine Lake is a large shield volcano whose highest summit elevation of 7,913 feet rises only about 4,000 feet above the surrounding Modoc Plateau. Low in height, but large in area, Medicine Lake Volcano is the largest in the Cascade Range. Medicine Lake itself, less than two miles long, lies within the volcano's 4.5- by 7.5-mile-wide caldera. The caldera is considered to have formed by subsidence when large volumes of basalt and andesite were erupted on the slopes of the volcano. In both shape and caldera origin, Medicine Lake Volcano appears more like a Hawaiian volcano than its Cascade sister-volcanoes.

▲ **Above:** *Blazing Star.*
▼ **Below:** *Glass Mountain,
a rhyolite to dacite flow
near the summit of
Medicine Lake Volcano, is
well named. Obsidian glass,
raw material for arrow-
heads and stone age
knives, is common here.
This flow, only about
1,000 years old, lies a
few miles south of Lava
Beds. Perhaps someday
this fascinating area will
be incorporated with-
in the monument.*

Lavas that built Medicine Lake Volcano range from basaltic to rhyolitic, with basalt and andesite predominating. Near the summit is a geologically young, steep-sided flow of rhyolite and dacite obsidian called Glass Mountain (7,622 feet). Radiocarbon dating indicates that this viscous flow was extruded only about 1,000 years ago. Seventeen eruptions of Medicine Lake Volcano have taken place during the past 13,000 years; eight of these clustered during an interval of a few hundred years, about 10,000 to 11,000 years ago, and poured out more than a cubic mile of basaltic lava. A small andesite eruption occurred about 4,300 years ago, and this was followed during the past 3,400 years by nine eruptions ranging from basalt to rhyolite, the latest being the Glass Mountain obsidian. Vents low on the volcano erupted mainly basalt, while the higher-silica dacite and rhyolite eruptions occurred near the summit. This number of eruptions for a Cascade Range volcano is second only to Mount St. Helens over the past few thousand years, and indicates that Medicine Lake Volcano has a high probability of future eruptions.

Most of the lava flows in Lava Beds National Monument are basaltic, the main one being the Mammoth Crater flow that erupted from several vents low on the volcano about 30,000 years ago. It is this flow that hosts most of the 300 lava-tube caves in the monu-

ment, and is one of the volcano's largest at nearly 100 square miles in area and more than one cubic mile in volume. All this apparently erupted during an interval of less than 100 years. That rate of eruption is comparable to the rate of the current, long-lived Pu'u O'o eruption of Kilauea volcano in Hawaii. The Mammoth Crater flows traveled more than 15 miles down the north slope of Medicine Lake Volcano, indicating that they were hot—about 2,100°F.—and of low viscosity, about the same as liquid honey. The formation of lava tubes also enabled the flows to travel long distances by preventing rapid cooling of the molten basalt.

Lava tubes are common in Hawaii, and recent eruptions have provided some insights into their formation and characteristics. They usually develop in pahoehoe lava flows—basaltic flows with smooth to ropy surfaces—and often extend for miles down slope from the vent area to the moving front of the flow. Think of a river in winter that freezes over, but whose water keeps moving beneath the ice; divert the river upstream and the water level drops until the stream is empty, leaving behind an ice-tunnel cave. Compared to a river, the slope of a lava flow is generally greater, and the overall flow is wider than the lava tunnels, which are generally just a few feet to tens of feet across; but the principle is the same. If the flow stops or is diverted at its vent, the tube drains and it becomes a sinuous, tunnel-like cave a few feet to tens of feet beneath the surface. Sometimes the surface crust over an active lava tube breaks and allows a startling view of the red-hot lava flowing inside the tube. Geologists in Hawaii call these "skylights," and they use them to help estimate the

▲ *Winter settles with firm resolve on Schonchin Butte, a cinder cone named for one of the leaders of the Modoc Indian War. Summer can bring severe heat to the high, volcanic Modoc Plateau.*

▲ *Entrance to one of the many lava-tube caves at Lava Beds. Most of the cave entrances (or exits) are places where the roof of a lava tube has collapsed and the pile of broken rock from the roof provides a sloping entrance to the cave. There are 430 known caves at the monument, ranging in size from a crawl space to 60 feet in width, and from hundreds to thousands of feet long.*

rate at which lava is flowing. For best results it takes two skylights on the same tube separated by several hundred feet. A geologist at the upper skylight throws in a log of wood that quickly catches on fire as it is swept along on the surface of the flow inside the tube. Another geologist below measures the time it takes the flaming log to pass by the lower skylight. If the diameter of the tube can be estimated, the volume of the flow per minute, as well as its velocity, can be roughly calculated.

Sometimes a pause in an eruption allows a lava tube to drain and a part of its roof to collapse. If the eruption restarts, the new lava rushing down the old tube may be backed up by the collapsed rocks and pour out of an older skylight or weak area up slope. These "breakouts" can be spectacular, and if they feed a new surface flow, a whole new generation of higher-level lava tubes may be created.

Lava, unlike water, "freezes" over a temperature range of a couple of hundred degrees. This allows the molten rock in an active lava tube to melt and erode its way slowly down into hardened flows beneath it. It can also melt some of its own roof rocks into "lavacicles," and its sides into glassy blobs that ooze down the walls. Because of the tendency of lava tubes to erode their way downward, there is often an empty space filled by hot gases above the molten flow surface. This leaves one or more lava-level marks seen in lava-tube caves once the molten lava drains away.

Louis Heller, National Archives

▲ *Three Modoc prisoners await trial after their capture in the Modoc War, 1873. Captain Jack, John Schonchin and two other Modoc leaders (none pictured here) were hanged, and the remainder of the tribe was exiled to a reservation in Oklahoma.*

Be sure to visit Mushpot Cave near the visitor center in Lava Beds National Monument. This lava-tube cave is over 700 feet long and has electrical lighting. There are many other accessible caves along Cave Loop Road and other nearby spur roads. For these you will need lanterns or flashlights, and a hard hat is advisable. Lights, hard hats, and good advice are available at the visitor center. We recommend Skull Cave, a large multi-level cave with ice at the bottom.

Mammoth Crater, one of the major vents of the huge lava flows which formed the tubes and covered most of the monument, is just a short walk off the road at the south border of the monument. Other interesting features in a younger flow are the Fleener Chimneys, spatter cones built of molten globs of lava that welded together as they fell from lava fountains and piled up around their vents. The 50-foot-deep "chimney" formed as the molten lava in the conduit receded when the eruption was over.

The rugged lava formations near the north border of the monument were the hideouts of Captain Jack, a Modoc Indian leader, and his 50 men, who held off the U.S. Army for 5 months during the winter and spring of 1873. The connection between Native Americans and Lava Beds National Monument doesn't just begin there. Long before the United States became a nation, American Indians carved hundreds of drawings into the soft rock formation at Petroglyph Point, where a tuff cone erupted beneath the water of once-higher Tule Lake.

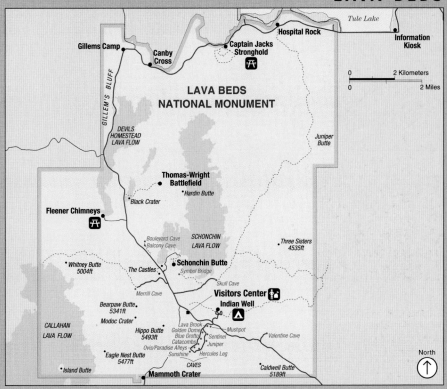

Map labels:
Tule Lake
Gillems Camp
Canby Cross
Captain Jacks Stronghold
Hospital Rock
Information Kiosk
GILLEM'S BLUFF
LAVA BEDS NATIONAL MONUMENT
DEVILS HOMESTEAD LAVA FLOW
Juniper Butte
Thomas-Wright Battlefield
Hardin Butte
Black Crater
Fleener Chimneys
Boulevard Cave
Balcony Cave
SCHONCHIN LAVA FLOW
Three Sisters 4535ft
Whitney Butte 5004ft
The Castles
Schonchin Butte
Symbol Bridge
Skull Cave
Merrill Cave
Visitors Center
Indian Well
Bearpaw Butte 5341ft
Modoc Crater
Lava Brook
Golden Dome
Mushpot
Valentine Cave
CALLAHAN LAVA FLOW
Hippo Butte 5493ft
Blue Grotto
Catacombs
Sentinel
Juniper
Ovis/Paradise Alleys
Eagle Nest Butte 5477ft
Sunshine
Hercules Leg
Island Butte
CAVES
Caldwell Butte 5189ft
Mammoth Crater
0 2 Kilometers
0 2 Miles
North

GETTING THERE

Lava Beds National Monument is in north-eastern California, 40 miles south of Klamath Falls, Oregon, via Oregon State Highway 39 and California State Highway 139; turn west at Tulelake, California. The nearest commercial airport is in Klamath Falls.

ESSENTIALS

There is a campground near the visitor center, and picnic areas at Fleener Chimneys and Captain Jacks Stronghold, but food, lodging, and gasoline are not available in the monument. Entrance fees are collected year round. The visitor center is open daily except Thanksgiving and Christmas.

CLIMATE

The 4,000- to 5,000-foot elevation on the Modoc Plateau sustains warm, dry summer days, sometimes interrupted by thunderstorms.

Winters are cold and windy. Temperatures at Medicine Lake, the summit area of the volcano eight miles south of the monument, drop to near-freezing even on some summer nights. Wear warm clothes, boots, and gloves for exploring the lava-tube caves.

INFORMATION

Lava Beds National Monument
Post Office Box 867
Indian Wells Headquarters
Tulelake, CA 96134
Telephone: 530-667-2282
Website: www.nps.gov/labe/

VOLCANO FACTS

Name – Medicine Lake Volcano
Volcano type – shield volcano with caldera
Rock types – basalt to rhyolite
Height – 7,913 feet
Latest eruption – about 950 years ago

167

DEVILS POSTPILE
NATIONAL MONUMENT, CALIFORNIA

Devils Postpile, a spectacular example of columnar basalt, is nestled in a deep valley along the upper reaches of the San Joaquin River at an elevation of 7,600 feet. Even though its official boundaries embrace little more than one square mile in area, the monument occupies the heart of a far larger Sierra Nevada wilderness region spiked by the 12,000- to 13,000-foot summits of the Ritter Range, including the spectacular Minarets, rising strikingly (as seen from the access road at Minaret Vista) above the valley's western edge.

The "Postpile" itself refers to the cliff composed of basalt columns, and the talus slope below made up of broken pieces of the columns, which look like giant fence posts. The short walk to the columns through the forest by the river (one mile round-trip) is a delight. Many of the columns appear nearly vertical, others decidedly warped. About 50 to 60 feet high, and one to two feet in diameter, they appear to have been chiseled by an expert rock carver. Many of them are six-sided, but a closer look reveals that some of the broken talus pieces have four and five sides, and occasionally three or seven. Be sure to climb the short trail that leads to the top of the cliff at Devils Postpile. Here you can see some remarkable glacial polish and striations—grooves cut into the basalt by rocks that were embedded in the bottom of the flowing glacier. Looking down on the horizontal surface planed off by the glacier, you can see the polygonal cracks that form the columns. They appear like a tile floor pattern.

Columnar basalts occur in other places in the world; the Giants Causeway in Ireland, and some lava cliffs along the Columbia River are good examples. In all the places where they are found, erosion has exposed the interior of thick lava flows, and this has led geologists to believe that the columns form inside the flows while they are cooling and hardening.

◄ *Opposite:* Columnar basalt creates this intriguing cliff named the Devils Postpile. Sometime less than 100,000 years ago, a basalt lava flow filled this deep Sierra valley on the upper San Joaquin River to a depth of 400 feet. As the thick flow slowly cooled, regular vertical cracks were formed by contraction. The most recent glacier that ground down the valley about 20,000 years ago tore away much of the solidified flow, exposing the columns.
▼ *Below:* The tops of the columns, polished like floor tiles by the glacier, show the mostly five- and six-sided pattern of the contraction process.

As molten rock solidifies it shrinks, and if the cooling is rapid, the shrinkage cracks are irregular. As a thick flow cools, however, it loses heat more slowly to the surface and into the cold rocks over which it flowed. The vertical shrinkage will be accommodated by settling, but the horizontal shrinkage will be taken up by vertical cracks that keep extending downward from the surface and upward from the bottom. This is a slow process; in a thick flow it may take many years, but the result of this slow, steady cooling is a network of vertical cracks that break the lava into columns. Sometimes the columns are curved, which indicates that the direction of heat loss was sideways rather than vertical. This might occur if the shape of the land over which the flow traveled was irregular, or if large amounts of water seeped into places in the cooling mass.

At Devils Postpile a thick basalt flow filled this part of the valley of the river to a depth of about 400 feet, at some time more recent than 100,000 years ago. The vent was a short distance upstream from the northern boundary of the monument. The flow occurred

▶ *Opposite:*
The San Joaquin River plunges 101 feet over a ledge of lava at Rainbow Falls, a pleasant hike downstream from the Devils Postpile cliff.

▼ *Below:* *Inyo Crater, a few miles east of Devils Postpile, erupted only about 600 years ago, and is one of the younger volcanic features in this region. Small pumice lumps from the explosion cloud of this crater cover the surface of the soil in the monument.*

sometime between the last two periods of glaciation. There are no Postpile basalt pieces in the debris from the next-to-last glacier that ground though the canyon 130,000 years ago, but there is ample evidence that the hardened flow was eroded and torn open by the last glacier some 20,000 years ago. Beautiful Rainbow Falls pours 101 feet down one exposed volcanic precipice downstream on the San Joaquin from the Postpile, and is accessible by a four-mile loop trail from the monument parking area.

This region east of the central Sierra Nevada has been an area of ongoing volcanism for the past three million years. The most notable eruption formed Long Valley 760,000 years ago, a caldera 20 miles long, 10 miles wide, and more than a mile deep. The town of Mammoth Lakes, inside the caldera, is only seven miles east of Devils Postpile. The Long Valley eruption expelled 175 cubic miles of pyroclastic deposits known as the Bishop Tuff, comparable to the great Yellowstone Caldera eruption 630,000 years ago.

Mammoth Mountain, a popular ski resort, is a complex volcano that grew on the southeast rim of the Long Valley Caldera from about 220,000 to 50,000 years ago. The road from Mammoth Lakes to Devils Postpile National Monument passes just north of Mammoth Mountain. The light gray pumice that overlies the soil in the monument was erupted from the Inyo and Mono Craters about 500 to 600 years ago. The latest eruption in the region, 250 years ago, occurred at Paoha Island in Mono Lake, 25 miles north of Devils Postpile. Even more recent has been the ongoing unrest of Long Valley Caldera, which began with a series of magnitude 6 earthquakes in 1980, but has not produced an eruption.

Will Devils Postpile erupt again? Probably not, but somewhere in the region, given enough time, another volcano almost certainly will. When? Scientists cannot yet answer that question.

▲ **Top and** ▼ **below:**
A common wildflower throughout many western national parks, lupine also thrives in the Sierra Nevada. Differing species of this versatile member of the pea family can grow as a bush or as singular stems, and can come in purple, blue, white and yellow.

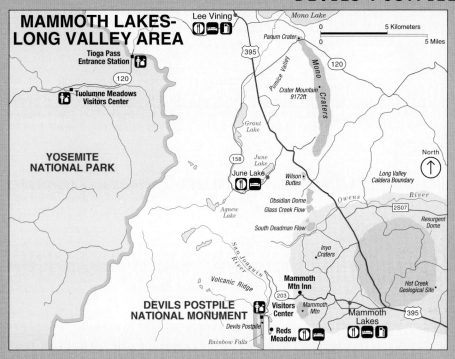

MAMMOTH LAKES-LONG VALLEY AREA

Lee Vining

Mono Lake

Tioga Pass
Entrance Station

120

Tuolumne Meadows
Visitors Center

YOSEMITE
NATIONAL PARK

Panum Crater

395

Pumice Valley

Crater Mountain
9172ft

Mono Craters

120

Grant
Lake

June
Lake

158

June Lake

Agnew
Lake

Wilson
Buttes

Obsidian Dome
Glass Creek Flow

South Deadman Flow

North

Long Valley
Caldera Boundary

Owens   River

2S07

Resurgent
Dome

San Joaquin River

Volcanic Ridge

DEVILS POSTPILE
NATIONAL MONUMENT

Devils Postpile

Rainbow Falls

Inyo
Craters

Mammoth
Mtn Inn

203

Visitors
Center

Mammoth
Mtn

Reds
Meadow

Mammoth
Lakes

Hot Creek
Geological Site

395

0   5 Kilometers
0   5 Miles

► GETTING THERE

Devils Postpile National Monument lies 17 miles west of US Highway 395 on dead-end State Highway 203 (Minaret Summit Road) in eastern California. There is a small commercial airport at the resort town of Mammoth Lakes, but the closest major airports are hundreds of miles away--at Los Angeles, Las Vegas, and (in summer, when State Highway 120 over Tioga Pass is open) San Francisco. During summer, visitors to the monument must ride the shuttle bus (fee) from Mammoth Mountain Inn from 7:30 a.m. to 5:30 p.m. Cars are not allowed on the steep road to the monument while shuttle buses are operating unless drivers have lodging reservations at Reds Meadow, or campground reservations in the monument or adjacent Inyo National Forest.

► ESSENTIALS

Devils Postpile is open only from late spring to early fall. There is a ranger station and a campground in the park, but food, lodging, and gasoline are not available. Reds Meadow, a summer resort two miles southeast, has food and lodging.

The monument does not charge an entrance fee, though visitors must pay a fare to ride the summer shuttle bus.

► CLIMATE

Warm summer days with cool to cold nights.

► INFORMATION

Devils Postpile National Monument
Post Office Box 501
Mammoth Lakes, California 93546
Telephone: 760-934-2289 (summer)
        or 760-872-4881 (winter)
Website: www.nps.gov/depo/

► VOLCANO FACTS

Name – Devils Postpile
Volcano type – thick lava flow with columnar joints
Rock type – basalt
Height – about 100 feet above the San Joaquin River
Last eruption – less than 100,000 years ago

173

DEATH VALLEY
NATIONAL PARK, CALIFORNIA

▼ *Below: At 280 feet below sea level, Badwater is almost the lowest spot in North America (the lowest, 282 feet below sea level, lies a few miles to the west). The water in the shallow pool is "bad" because it is extremely salty, but it is not poisonous.*

▶ *Opposite:*

The Panamint Range, seen across Death Valley from Furnace Creek Inn, soars to 11,049 feet at its highest point, Telescope Peak. This landscape is still forming, as forces in the Earth pull apart this region of California.

This huge desert and mountain park in southeastern California is a geologist's dream. The stories told in its rocks extend back more than a billion years and, thanks to the lack of soil and vegetation, these stories in stone are clearly visible, if not completely understood. Basically, Death Valley was formed by the down-dropping of a great block of land between mountain ranges that have been uplifted. This basin-and-range faulting began about 14 million years ago, and continues today. Thousands of feet of sediments fill the valley, but subsidence outpaces the filling. Some 500 square miles of its floor are below sea level; the deepest place, near Badwater, is minus 282 feet in elevation. Telescope Peak, only a few miles west of Badwater, is 11,049 feet high, making the eastern escarpment of the Panamint Range an imposing mountain wall that rises more than two miles above the white salt flats of Death Valley.

▲ **Above:** *Ubehebe Crater is a half-mile wide and 600 feet deep. A few thousand years ago great explosive volcanic eruptions blasted out the crater when molten rock rose along fractures and mixed with ground water. The superheated water flashed to steam, blowing out rocks and cinders.*

▼ **Below:** *Cotton-top cactus.*

Rugged mountains, sand dunes, salt flats, extreme summer temperatures, old mining ventures; if only there were volcanoes in Death Valley. Ah, but there are! Ubehebe Crater and several smaller craters, 55 miles north of Furnace Creek Visitor Center, are young explosion vents that were excavated by steam explosions when rising basaltic magma encountered groundwater in the gravel and sand layers of the valley fill. The Shoshone Indian name for Ubehebe Crater is Tempintta Wosah, meaning "Basket in the Rock," an excellent descriptive name for this steep-walled crater, half a mile wide and 600 feet deep. The colored rocks in the crater wall are the hardened gravel and sand layers through which the volcano exploded, and the dark gray layers overlying them are the basaltic cinders and ash that fell back from the explosion clouds.

The overall shape of Ubehebe is a low-relief cone dominated by the central crater. The outer slopes of the cone are covered for several square miles by fall-back of ash and cinders, but the climb to the crater is much less steep than on a typical cinder cone. This type of volcano is known as a tuff ring, and if the explosion crater is filled with water it is called a maar. A group of smaller craters south of Ubehebe appears to have formed first, then a western cluster followed by Ubehebe, the largest crater, and Little Hebe. The age of these volcanoes has been estimated at about 1,000 to 3,000 years, but a recent radiocarbon date suggests the youngest eruption from the group may be only 200 to 300 years old. There is a steep but easy trail from the rim of Ubehebe to the crater bottom. The climb back up, especially on a hot day, is by no means easy. The trail around the rim, which passes by the smaller crater of Little Hebe, is more scenic.

The Ubehebe craters are the youngest but not the only volcanic features in the park. The central Death Valley volcanic field has been intermittently active along the sides of the valley for 12 million years as the early sedimentary basins began to subside. Volcanic ash layers and occasional lava flows are interbedded with the lake-basin sediments that have been upturned

▼ Artist's Palette looks as if it had been painted with a giant brush, but the colors really were supplied by nature. Some, like the violets and greens, are formed by the alteration of minerals in the volcanic ash, while the reds, yellows and browns are from iron minerals that commonly occur in rust.

▲ **Above:** *Cholla cactus.*
▼ **Below:** *Cinder Hill, a 700,000-year-old cinder cone, grew over an earthquake fault in Death Valley. Accumulated movement on the fault has displaced the west side of the cone 600 feet to the north.*

along the east side of the valley near Furnace Creek. The famous colored rock formations at Artist's Palette are volcanic ash beds stained by the oxidation of iron, manganese, and other minerals contained in the ash.

The most recent eruptions from this volcanic field have not been dated, but since extension and subsidence of Death Valley are still ongoing, it will not be surprising if future eruptions occur. Two dark reddish-brown cinder and spatter cones can be seen near the base of the Panamint Range as you look across the valley near Furnace Creek. These cones are slowly being buried by the growing alluvial fans—slopes of sand and gravel—that wash down from the Panamints during flash floods.

A unique basaltic cinder cone called Cinder Hill occurs in southern Death Valley. This 700,000 year old volcano grew on top of the surface break of the Southern Death Valley Fault—

presumably the fracture acted as a conduit for magma rising to the surface. Movements on the fault since the eruption of the cinder cone have displaced the west side of the cone more than 600 feet in a northerly direction.

Warm springs in the hills east of Furnace Creek village flow at about 1,000 gallons per minute, and provide the water for this desert oasis. The water is rich in calcium carbonate, and has deposited travertine layers near the spring openings. The warmth of the water is probably due to its deep circulation underground rather than heating by any volcanic roots. There are hot springs in Saline Valley, northwest of Death Valley but still within the park. The water here may be heated by shallow underground intrusions of magma that have not yet completely cooled.

Death Valley is certainly not dead when it comes to geologic activity like earthquakes and volcanoes. Fortunately for the tranquillity of this beautiful, vast and nearly empty park, the time intervals between major quakes and eruptions is on the order of hundreds to thousands of years.

▲ **Above:** *The view from Zabriskie Point shows the soft rock layers that were deposited by a prehistoric lake. The lighter colors–yellows, tans and browns--are mostly from iron minerals exposed to air. The darker layers–gray-green to dark gray–are volcanic ash and lava flows.*

▼ **Below:** *Desert rocknettle.*

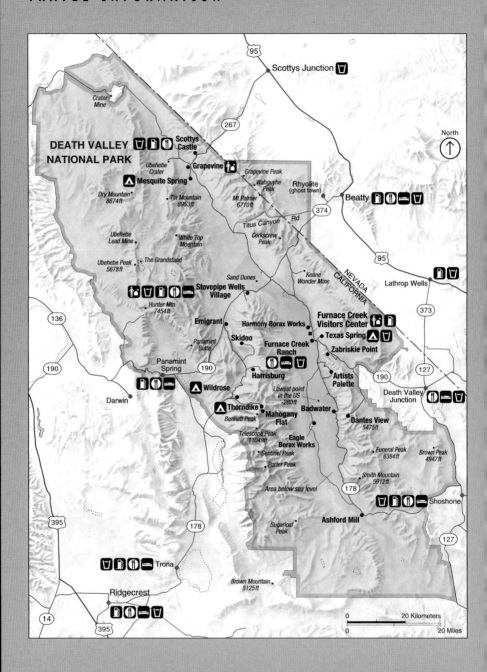

DEATH VALLEY
NATIONAL PARK

Scottys Junction

95

267

Crater
Mine

Scottys
Castle

Ubehebe
Crater

Grapevine

Grapevine Peak

Wahguyhe
Peak

Rhyolite
(ghost town)

Beatty

374

Mesquite Spring

Dry Mountain
8674ft

Tin Mountain
8953ft

Mt Palmer
6710ft

Titus Canyon   Rd

95

Ubehebe
Lead Mine

White Top
Mountain

Corkscrew
Peak

NEVADA
CALIFORNIA

Lathrop Wells

Ubehebe Peak
5678ft

The Grandstand

Sand Dunes

Keane
Wonder Mine

373

136

Stovepipe Wells
Village

Hunter Mtn
7454ft

Emigrant

Harmony Borax Works

Furnace Creek
Visitors Center

190

Panamint
Butte

Skidoo

Furnace Creek
Ranch

Texas Spring

Zabriskie Point

190

Panamint
Spring

190

Harrisburg

Artists
Palette

127

Death Valley
Junction

Darwin

Wildrose

Lowest point
in the US
-280ft

Badwater

190

Thorndike

Bennett Peak

Mahogany
Flat

Dantes View
5475ft

395

Telescope Peak
11049ft

Eagle
Borax Works

Funeral Peak
6384ft

Brown Peak
4947ft

Sentinel Peak

Porter Peak

Smith Mountain
5912ft

178

Area below sea level

Shoshone

Sugarloaf
Peak

Ashford Mill

127

Trona

Brown Mountain
5125ft

Ridgecrest

14

395

178

North

↑

0   20 Kilometers
0   20 Miles

DEATH VALLEY NATIONAL PARK

▸ **GETTING THERE**

Death Valley National Park is located in southeastern California on the Nevada border (in fact a small area of the park is in Nevada), about a two and one-half hour drive from Las Vegas, Nevada, via US Highway 95 (north), and Nevada State Highway 373 (west). From Los Angeles, California, the park is about a four-hour drive via Interstate 15 to Baker, north on California State Highway 127 to California State Highway 190, then west to Furnace Creek. There is a small airport at Furnace Creek, but no scheduled flights.

▸ **ESSENTIALS**

Food, lodging, and gasoline are available at Furnace Creek, Stove Pipe Wells, and Panamint Springs Resort, and there is a snack bar at Scotty's Castle. Visitors can camp year-round. The Furnace Creek Visitor Center has a museum and informative talks. Entrance fees are collected year round. The park is open day and night all year.

▸ **CLIMATE**

Elevation ranges from below sea level to over 11,000 feet. Average rainfall in the valley is about two inches per year, and summer temperatures may exceed 130°F., making fall and spring the most comfortable times to visit. Winter temperatures in the valley sometimes dip below freezing at night, and snow accumulates at the higher elevations. Hikers should wear sturdy shoes and sun protection, and carry lots of drinking water.

▸ **INFORMATION**

Death Valley National Park
Post Office Box 579
Death Valley, CA 92328-0579
Telephone: 760-786-2331
Website: www.nps.gov/deva/

▸ **VOLCANO FACTS**

Name – Ubehebe Crater
Volcano type – tuff ring or maar
Rock type – basalt
Height – a few hundred feet
　　　　　above surrounding terrain
Last eruption – about 1,000 years ago?

Beavertail cactus.

MOJAVE

Mojave National Preserve, like Death Valley National Park, is a geologist's dream come true. With stories told in the rocks that go back more than two billion years, and bare-bones rock outcrops created by ongoing mountain-building and the desert climate, geologists are piecing together the region's long and complex past. That prehistory includes both violence and tranquility, volcanic eruptions and erosion, and warm shallow seas filled with coral reefs. The vast landscape that remains is an adventurers' paradise—basin and range mountains, caves, a mysterious landscape feature called Cima Dome, granite tors, sand dunes, and volcanoes.

Two episodes of volcanic activity are particularly interesting, and their remains are easy to visit. The great explosive eruptions of the Woods Mountains volcanic center near Hole-in-the-Wall, in the southern half of the park, took place about 17 to 18 million years ago, which puts these huge explosions into the "ancient fires" category. In contrast, the more than thirty cinder cones and surrounding lava flows in the northwestern section near Baker, California, are much younger, having been erupted intermittently over the past eight million years, with the latest about 10,000 years ago. Since another cinder-cone eruption from this geologically young volcanic field is likely to occur during the next 100,000 years, we put this area in the "sleeping volcanoes" category.

The violence of the Woods Mountains eruptions can hardly be exaggerated. They began about 18 million years ago with explosions of pyroclastic flows, extrusions of lava domes, and flows of viscous rhyolite. After a pause, renewed explosions poured out a thick blanket of pyroclastic flows that covered more than 200 square miles with deposits hundreds of feet thick, now known as the Wildhorse Mesa Tuff. Many big blocks of rock from the vent areas, some as large as 60 feet across, were

◄ *Opposite: This vast swath of parkland in the eastern Mojave Desert encompasses rugged valleys and scores of dry mountain ranges, some of which reach more than 7,000 feet in elevation.*

▼ *Below: The spectacular bloom of the Joshua Tree is often one foot long. The forest of Joshua Trees near Cima Dome is the largest in the world.*

hurled out or swept along for miles by the hot, fragmental flows. Everything in the path of these high-speed, devastating pyroclastic flows was blown down and incinerated, and the heat was so intense that the loose fragments of ash and pumice were welded into solid rock when the flows finally stopped. As the magma that fed the violent pyroclastic flows was removed from beneath their vents, the surface of the ground collapsed into a gigantic caldera. This structure, now known as the Woods Mountains Caldera, has been broken by basin-and-range faulting and millions of years of erosion. Without geologic mapping, it is hardly recognizable as a caldera.

The rock outcrops called Hole-in-the-Wall, as well as the mesa to the northwest, are part of this thick deposit of welded Wildhorse Mesa Tuff. A fascinating and fun area to explore, the Hole-in-the-Wall resembles a jumbled mountain of stone reamed through and through with thousands of holes, many big enough to crawl through. A short trail from the Hole-in-the-Wall Visitor Center descends Banshee Canyon, a narrow cleft in the formation, which drops so sharply that hikers have to lower themselves down some sections with the aid of iron rings bolted to the rock face. Banshee Canyon widens at the bottom to form a strange amphitheater, which opens on the southwest into Wild Horse Canyon.

The cinder-cone field near Baker is more easily recognized as volcanic in origin because it is geologically younger—the latest eruption occurred about 10,000 years ago—and because it has not been as disrupted by faulting and erosion as the older volcanic rocks near Hole-in-the-Wall. In addition, the low rainfall of this desert region, and the high porosity of the cinder cones that allows the little rain that does fall to soak in rather than to run off, has preserved many of the youngest cones in nearly their original shapes. Some look as if they erupted just last year.

Most of the more than thirty cinder cones are from 100 to 300 feet high, and are surrounded by dark basalt lava flows that issued from vents near the bases of the cones. It appears that most, but not all, of the cones and adjacent flows were created during short-duration eruptions that lasted only a few months to a few years (see the description of the eruption of Parícutin Volcano in Mexico on pages 212-215). These brief eruptions were then followed by long periods of rest—thousands of years—until a new eruptive vent added another cone and flow to the overall volcanic field. In general, the younger cones are in the southern part of this 50

▼ **Below:** *After a wet winter, the early spring wildflowers (including the desert poppies shown here) can be fantastic. This is desert country, however, so be prepared for the unique beauty inherent in rocks, sand and dried-up vegetation.*

square mile area, and if future eruptions occur—as they probably will—they are likely to be in this southern section. "Probably" and "likely"—also "possibly"— are favorite terms of geologists trying to see into the future.

The paved road from Baker to Kelso, the "Kelbaker Road," cuts through one of the basalt flows and passes only about two miles south of three cinder cones. A cross-country hike over the rough but fairly flat surface of a lava flow will take you to the base of one of these cinder cones. Climbing the cinder cone provides a real example of "angle of repose." For three steps up, you slide two steps back, but from the top you will see the crater and a good view of this major volcanic field. If you had been on the rim of this cinder cone during its eruption, you would have been severely pelted by the hot but solid fragments of lava—the "cinders"—as they fell from the lava fountain spraying from the crater.

Another igneous-rock feature of Mojave Preserve is the mysterious Cima Dome, a nearly perfect, gently rounded dome that rises about 1,500 feet across a width of 10 miles. Its shape is like a giant

▲ **Above:** *The "trail" down Banshee Canyon to Wild Horse Canyon at Hole-in-the-Wall is aided by iron rings installed into the rock. The rock formation is Wild Horse Mesa Tuff, a pyroclastic flow deposit blasted from the nearby Woods Mountains caldera about 16 to 17 million years ago.*

billiard ball about 90 percent buried below the surface. Although composed of granite, it is not at all like the steep domes in Yosemite National Park. Cima Dome is covered with a forest of Joshua Trees, and its slopes are so gradual that they are nearly imperceptible. The dome is best seen in profile at a distance from vistas along the Cedar Canyon Road, to the northwest.

Cima Dome is an eroded granite pluton, the crystallized rock of a large, deeply-buried chamber of molten magma that fed a chain of volcanoes some 100 to 150 million years ago. The volcanic chain has been eroded away; only its hardened granite roots remain. Like Yosemite National Park, this "volcanic" feature is only preserved by the remains of its ancient fires.

The origin of the gentle topographic bulge of Cima Dome is still argued by geologists. Most who have studied it think it results from a long period of desert erosion that has reduced a mountain area that was once much more rugged into this wide gentle dome. Others are not sure how it came to be.

◄ *Opposite:* Sand blown across Devil's Playground from the Mojave River Sink deposited the Kelso Dunes, one of the largest dune fields in the American West.

▼ *Below:* A young Joshua Tree, a yucca, and a cholla cactus stand guard in the vast empty desert. In the background are several cinder cones of the more than 30 that dot this region of the preserve south of Baker. The youngest eruption in this cinder cone field is estimated to have happened about 10,000 years ago.

Jeff Nicholas

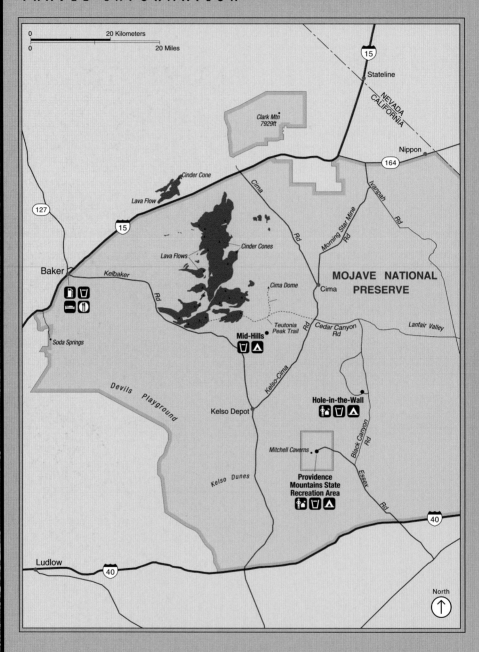

MOJAVE NATIONAL PRESERVE

▶ GETTING THERE

Mojave National Preserve is a huge, 2,500-square-mile desert wilderness in Southern California, 150 miles northeast of Los Angeles, CA, and 60 miles southwest of Las Vegas, NV, the closest major airports. It is bounded on the north by Interstate Highway 15, and on the south by Interstate Highway 40.

▶ ESSENTIALS

There are Mojave Information Centers in Baker and Needles, California, a seasonal visitor center at Hole-in-the-Wall, and the Desert Information Center at Barstow, all in California. Two maintained campgrounds are available, but there is no lodging. Motels, gas, and supplies are available in Baker on the northwest boundary, and there are small stores at Cima and Nipton. No fees or back-country permits are required.

▶ CLIMATE

Elevations in this desert area vary from 1,000 to 8,000 feet. Summers are very hot, and winters cold, sometimes freezing. The best seasons to visit are spring or fall.

▶ INFORMATION

Mojave National Preserve
222 E. Main Street, Suite 202
Barstow, CA 92311
Telephones: 760-733-4040 (Baker)
760-326-6322 (Needles)
760-255-8801 (Barstow)
Website: www.nps.gov/moja

▶ VOLCANO FACTS

Name – Cinder Cones
Volcano type – cinder cones
 with surrounding lava flows
Rock type – basalt
Height – 100 to 300 feet above surrounding 1,500 – to 3,000-foot elevation
Latest eruption – about 10,000 years ago

Name – Woods Mountains Volcanic Center
Volcano type – caldera and widespread pyroclastic flows
Rock type – rhyolite
Last eruption – about 16 million years ago

Above: *Desert mallow.*
Below: *Mojave mound cactus.*

CRATERS OF THE MOON
NATIONAL MONUMENT, IDAHO

Before satellites and men circled and landed on the moon in the 1960s, there were lively scientific arguments as to whether the moon craters were of volcanic or meteorite-impact origin. That question is now settled; although there are many lava flows on the moon, most of the craters were formed by impact, billions of years ago.

The Craters of the Moon in Idaho, however, are definitely of volcanic origin. They and their associated lava flows are geologically young, having erupted between 15,000 and 2,000 years ago. That youth and the dry climate of the region make many of these volcanic features appear as if they were created only a few decades ago.

The 83 square miles of the original monument contain many of the youngest and most easily accessible cones, craters, and flows of the 618 square-mile Craters of the Moon lava field. The basaltic lavas of this field have erupted from the "Great Rift," a zone of northwest-southeast fractures about one to three miles wide and sixty miles long that cuts across the Snake River Plain of southern Idaho. In November, 2000, President Clinton added 1,033 square miles of land to the monument so that it now incorpates nearly all of the young lava field.

The Snake River Plain is itself of volcanic origin, the rocks beneath it date back as much as 15 million years, and its fertile soils grow the famous Idaho potatoes. Four hundred miles long and 40 to 80 miles wide, the eastern Snake River Plain is considered by most geologists to have formed in the wake of the Yellowstone Hot Spot (see pages 197-198). It is composed of flood basalts underlain by rhyolitic volcanic rocks, and their ages in general become younger from west to east. The Craters of the Moon lava field lies near the center of the eastern Snake River Plain, and overlies flows that are millions of years older. Its young geologic age remains a mystery.

Words describing a first impression of Craters of the Moon include *strange, barren, weird, bleak,* and *monotonous,* but also *exciting, awe-inspiring, astonishing, curious, colorful,* and *mysterious.* We subscribe to the second group; if one can imagine the fiery origin of

▼ *From early May until summer, wildflowers (including this Blazing Star bloom) add touches of softness and color to the otherwise hard-edged, somber-colored lava fields.*

D.R. Clark, NPS

this place, and appreciate the way Nature has slowly colonized it with plants and animals, it is a place of great beauty. Out of this world, perhaps, but that is part of its mystery.

The monument is an outdoor laboratory of volcanology and ecology. Within the area there are about 25 cinder cones, 60 lava flows and 10 fissures, many with spatter cones. The cinder cones grow by the fall-back of fragments of lava around fiery fountains that spray clots of molten lava hundreds of feet into the air. The clots cool and harden in flight and accumulate near the vent in steep-sided piles of volcanic cinders. Finer particles called volcanic ash are blown downwind and cover large areas beyond the base of the cones. Occasionally a larger blob of lava was hurled from an erupting vent, partly cooling to form a volcanic bomb. These bombs lie scattered on the sides and base of some cinder cones. Big Cinder Butte, 750 feet high, is the tallest cinder cone in the monument.

Eruptions that take place along fissures generate "curtains of fire," continuous chains of lava fountains that generally spout less high than fountains from single vents. The lava clots falling from these less vigorous fountains are still molten and weld themselves to earlier-fallen lava blobs. Such mounds are called spatter cones, or if continuous along the fissure they are named spatter ramparts.

▲ *Rising 750 feet above the surrounding lava beds, Big Cinder Butte is one of the higher summits flanking the northern end of the Great Rift Zone, where most of the monument roads and facilities are concentrated.*

Some cinder cones are ancient weathervanes. The rim of the crater that was downwind when the lava fountain was erupting becomes the highest point. A symmetrical cone and crater suggest that the fountain was vertical and winds were calm. Sometimes cinder cones are horseshoe-shaped; this occurs when a lava flow issuing from the base of the cone rafts away a sector of the pile. Large chunks of the cone that are carried away by the flow will often be broken into large blocks that stand above the general flow surface. The Devils Orchard formed in this manner.

Several of the lava flows at Craters of the Moon were large and traveled for tens of miles from their vents over fairly flat ground. This indicates they were hot—about 2,100°F.—and fluid—about the viscosity of liquid honey. There are both pahoehoe and a'a flows, the latter where the flows had cooled and become more viscous, but were still moving. The eight periods of volcanic eruption at Craters of the Moon generally lasted less than a few hundred years each, and were separated by dormant periods of a few hundred to a few thousand years. Will the area erupt again? Probably. When? No one knows, but the length of time it has presently been sleeping, about 2,000 years, is roughly the same as some of its previous dormant intervals.

▼ **Below:** The half-mile, self-guiding Devils Orchard Nature Trail takes hikers to an "island" of lava formations jutting up through surrounding beds of cinders.

Ron Warfield

Plants and animals in the monument prove that you are not on the surface of the moon. The way in which they have colonized and found favorable niches in which to survive is the living side of this story. High on the south to southwest sides of the youngest cones only barren cinders face the heat of summer sun and the dry prevailing winds. In June on the lower slopes small wildflower gardens appear with several varieties including dwarf buckwheat and bitterroot. Grasses and small shrubs grow on the more sheltered and shaded middle slopes of the east, west, and north sides of the cone, and scattered limber pines appear on the lower northern slopes.

On the hard surfaces of young lava flows, lichens are among the first plants to appear. These algae and fungus colonies speed the slow process of decomposition of rock into soil. Plants need soil, be it volcanic ash, cinders, or decomposed rock, and the dying plant remains add organic matter to the slowly improving soil. Once plants become established there are seeds, fruits, and forage for animals. On a land that is only 2,000 years old, there is already a sparse but complex food chain and web of life.

Plan at least half a day for seeing Craters of the Moon. Stop at the visitor center, and then drive the seven-mile-loop road. A short trail at the parking area at North Crater Flow leads to good examples of pahoehoe and a'a lava flows. A half-mile loop trail at Devils Orchard leads through wonderful wildflowers growing in the cinders in springtime.

▲ Among the more unusual forms that lava takes at Craters of the Moon is the iridescent blue surface of the Blue Dragon lava flow **(top left)**, which formed about 2,100 years ago, and takes its hue from titanium magnetite microcrystals in its glassy surface. Solidified lava channels **(upper right)** contrast with the ropy pahoehoe lava-flow surface **(lower right)**, both of which are identical to similar flow features in Hawaii.

▼ **Below:** The red fox shares the lava beds with 46 other mammal species and eight kinds of reptiles.

D. R. Clark, NPS

▲ **Above:** Desert paintbrush.

▼ **Below:** Ranger-guided walks introduce visitors to the fascinating geological wonders of the park, including some of the many lava-tube caves that underlie the lava beds.

At Inferno Cone parking area, a short but steep trail leads to a great viewpoint on top of the cone. From here the alignment of cones and vents along the Great Rift can be clearly seen. From Big Craters and Spatter Cones you can see several spatter vents very close to the parking area.

A spur road to the right from the loop leads to fine examples of tree molds, where trees buried by lava left their impressions cast in stone when they later burned or rotted out. From Cave Area, a half-mile-long trail leads to several lava-tube caves. Flashlights are needed except in Indian Tunnel, which has so many skylights in its roof that extra light is not needed.

Consider stopping again at the visitor center as you leave the monument. Experts inside may be able to answer any questions your outdoor laboratory has raised, and a second look at the exhibits may help tie together what you have seen. One of the best lessons from young volcanic landscapes is seeing that life eventually recovers from destruction.

CRATERS OF THE MOON

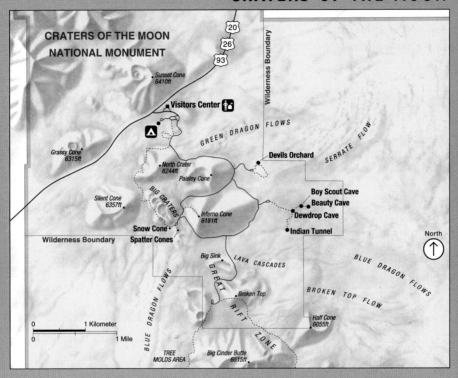

CRATERS OF THE MOON
NATIONAL MONUMENT

20
26
93

Sunset Cone
6410ft

■ Visitors Center

Grassy Cone
6315ft

GREEN DRAGON FLOWS

Devils Orchard

SERRATE FLOW

North Crater
6244ft
Paisley Cone

Boy Scout Cave
Beauty Cave
Dewdrop Cave
Indian Tunnel

Silent Cone
6357ft

BIG CRATERS

Inferno Cone
6181ft

Snow Cone
Spatter Cones

Wilderness Boundary

Wilderness Boundary

Big Sink

LAVA CASCADES

North

BLUE DRAGON FLOWS

0   1 Kilometer
0   1 Mile

GREAT

Broken Top

BROKEN TOP FLOW

RIFT

Half Cone
6055ft

BLUE DRAGON FLOWS

ZONE

TREE
MOLDS AREA

Big Cinder Butte
6515ft

▶ **GETTING THERE**

Craters of the Moon National Monument is in southern Idaho, 18 miles west of Arco on US Highway 93. There is scheduled air service to Idaho Falls, 87 miles east.

▶ **ESSENTIALS**

Entrance fees are collected year round. There is no lodging, food service, or gasoline available in the monument, though there is a campground with water. The visitor center, open daily except for fall, winter, and spring holidays, has snack and soda machines. Loop road is closed from about November 1 to April 15, but is groomed for cross-country skiing in winter. Snowmobiles are not permitted.

▶ **CLIMATE**

Elevation ranges from 5,300 to 7,700 feet, with warm to hot, dry summers, and cold winters with moderate snowfall. Average July temperatures range from 84° to 51°F; and January from 29° to 10°F.

▶ **INFORMATION**

Craters of the Moon National Monument
Post Office Box 29
Arco, ID 83213
Telephone: 208-527-3257
Website: www.nps.gov/crmo

▶ **VOLCANO FACTS**

Name – Craters of the Moon volcanic field
Volcano types – fissure eruptions with
                        cinder and spatter cones
Rock type – basalt
Height – cinder cones 100 to 700 feet
              above surrounding plains
Latest eruption – about 2,000 years ago

YELLOWSTONE
NATIONAL PARK, WYOMING, MONTANA & IDAHO

Historians disagree on how the Yellowstone River—and thereby the park—got its name. It derives from a Minnetaree Indian name that translates to "Yellow Stone," but it is not clear whether the original Indian name referred to the yellowish sandstone bluffs along the river near Billings, Montana, or to the decayed yellow rocks in the deep canyon now known as the Grand Canyon of the Yellowstone—rocks of volcanic origin (see page 45). Of course we prefer to think that our first national park was named for its volcanic scenery.

Most people recognize Old Faithful Geyser as the most familiar feature of Yellowstone National Park, but few realize that Old Faithful is a clue that Yellowstone is a great volcano, one of the world's largest. The underground heat escaping from this sleeping giant, mainly through Yellowstone's unrivaled hot springs and geysers, is about thirty times the normal heat flow from the Earth's surface.

What furnace fires this great volcano and its geothermal features? Geologists call it the Yellowstone Hot Spot. Although this hot spot has been active for more than 16 million years, the concept of a geological hot spot has evolved only during the past 40 years. Basically the idea is that there are slowly rising plumes of hot but solid rock in the Earth's mantle that partially melt to generate magma as the plumes move up into the lower pressures in the upper mantle. The melting temperature of most materials, rock included, is lowered as the surrounding pressure is decreased. There are some thirty geological hot spots on Earth (depending on who is counting), and one of the best known besides Yellowstone is the Hawaiian Hot Spot that created the entire Hawaiian Island chain.

As one of Earth's tectonic plates moves slowly over a relatively stationary hot spot, it is marked by a trail of ancient volcanoes that indicate the direction of the plate motion. The dead volcanoes are progressively older away from the active volcanic center that lies directly over the hot spot. If the ages of the older volcanoes can be established, the rate of motion of the plate can then be determined. In the case of the

◄ *Opposite*: Mounds of sinter around their vents have inspired many geyser names like "Grotto" and (shown here) Castle Geyser. Mats of bacteria color the hot to warm water in the runoff channels.

▼ *Below*: Old Faithful Inn, a historic hotel built of logs and stone in 1904, stands cold and empty in winter. In summer this bustling inn, with a classic view of Old Faithful Geyser, is a wonderful place to stay.

Yellowstone Hot Spot, the North American Plate appears to be moving southwest over it at a rate of one inch per year. About 16 million years ago, the Yellowstone Hot Spot was beneath the area that is now the junction of the states of Idaho, Oregon, and Nevada. Today, the hot spot lies beneath Yellowstone Park, or perhaps just northeast of it. The Snake River Plain, the topographic feature between the junction of the three states and Yellowstone, is the path made by the motion of the plate passing slowly over the hot spot. Not all geologists agree with the hot spot plume theory, but it appears to gain more supporters year by year.

One thing all the geologists who have studied Yellowstone do agree on is that during the past two million years it has had three huge volcanic eruptions, and many smaller ones. The main three were gigantic; the biggest bang, two million years ago, expelled 600 cubic miles of ash-fall and pyroclastic-flow deposits. Most of the flow deposits were so hot and thick that they consolidated into a hard, compact rock called welded tuff. The second, 1.3 million years ago, erupted about 70 cubic miles of similar debris. The third, 630 thousand years ago, spewed out an additional 240 cubic miles.

All three were huge eruptions of rhyolite, the volcanic rock that is chemically equivalent to granite. If granitic magma cools slowly underground, it hardens into coarsely crystalline granite; if it erupts

▶ *Opposite: The Grand Canyon of the Yellowstone River. The reddish yellow walls of the canyon are the result of hydrothermal alteration of rhyolitic volcanic rocks. The Minnetaree Indian name for the river translates to "Yellow Stone." Could the name of America's most famous national park have come from the volcanic coloring process seen here?*

▼ *Below: The rim of Yellowstone caldera north of Madison Junction as seen from the air. The floor of this gigantic caldera, in the foreground, sank as magma erupted from beneath it during a huge explosive eruption 630,000 years ago.*

to the surface, it cools rapidly and hardens into finely crystalline or glassy rhyolite. The combined volume of more than 900 cubic miles of rock and ash is a number so large that it is difficult to comprehend. It is roughly 5,000 times more than the volume of the 1980 eruption of Mount St. Helens, and is enough to bury all of Wyoming beneath a layer 50 feet thick.

Huge calderas formed by collapse as each of these giant explosive eruptions partly emptied their magma chambers. The first caldera eruption at Yellowstone, two million years ago, created a huge basin 50 miles long, 40 miles wide, and thousands of feet deep. The second, 1.3 million years ago, created a more circular hole in the ground, 15 miles wide and thousands of feet deep, called the Henry's Fork or Island Park caldera, which lies some 20 miles west of Yellowstone Park. The third, 630 thousand years ago, formed the present Yellowstone caldera, 45 miles long, 30 miles wide, and thousands of feet deep, that occupies much of the central and southern portions of the park. For thousands of years after each collapse, smaller eruptions of mainly rhyolite flows have partly filled the calderas. This and many ice-age glacial erosion cycles have obscured the original shape of the giant basins, so don't expect to see a giant Crater Lake-type caldera.

The latest eruptions in Yellowstone produced the thick rhyolite flows of the Pitchstone Plateau in the southeast part of the park, about 70,000 years ago. But Yellowstone's volcanoes are only sleeping; the great energy output from inside the Earth beneath Yellowstone is equal to the electric energy needed by a city of two million people. The myriad geysers and hot springs for which the park is so famous prove that the sleeping giant still has a high temperature, and occasional swarms of small earthquakes indicate that he is not entirely placid.

American Indians were familiar with the thermal features of Yellowstone. Arrowheads and other relics have been found at Mammoth Hot Springs and in the geyser basins, and legends linger of wars among spirits that create the steaming fountains. John Colter, a member of the 1804-1806 Lewis and Clark expedition that passed north of Yellowstone, returned in 1807 to trap beaver in the region and was the first person of European descent to see the geysers. He referred to them as "hot spring brimstone," and his tales of these thermal features to fellow trappers led to early interest in the area.

Dynamic evidence of volcanic activity abounds at Yellowstone, where two excellent (though often crowded) loop roads tour the primary geothermal basins and scenic wonders. From the eroded yellow rocks of the Yellowstone River's magnificent Grand Canyon, to the

◀ *Overleaf:*
Castle Geyser spouts off along the Firehole River in the Upper Geyser Basin. A quarter of all geysers on Earth are scattered through this basin in an area smaller than one square mile.
Don Pitcher

◀ *Opposite: The world's most famous geyser is arguably Old Faithful, which spouts nearly 100,000 pounds of boiling water and steam roughly every hour.*

myriad of mud pots, fumeroles, mineralized springs, geyser cones, hot springs, obsidian cliffs, petrified forests, hoodoos, and palisades, Yellowstone National Park is a grand museum of Nature's volcanic works. If there is one feature that stands out most for volcanolgists in Yellowstone, however, it is the abundance of thermal features, especially geysers, which are among the world's rarest of natural geothermal features. The ways in which geysers and hot springs work are discussed in pages 40-49, so here we will only briefly describe a few of Yellowstone's many examples in various places around the park.

Old Faithful, the archetype geyser, is the obvious place to start. Not only is it eminently beautiful, but it is easily accessible. Its eruptions of steam and hot water can be seen from Old Faithful Inn, from benches at Old Faithful Visitor Center, and from many scenic spots along boardwalk trails that invite the visitor to view it from both sides of the Firehole River. It erupts on average about every 80 minutes, spouting a brilliant white column of steam and hot water to heights of 100 to 180 feet. The eruption lasts for two to five minutes, shooting about 10,000 to 12,000 gallons of hot water into the air. Because of its beauty and ease of access, more people have witnessed its eruptions

than any other geyser on Earth. About three million people visit Yellowstone National Park every year, and most of them see one or more eruptions of Old Faithful. We don't think a single one of them is disappointed by this wondrous show of Nature.

The low hill at the site of Old Faithful is built up of siliceous sinter, a grayish white mineral that precipitates from the hot water as it cools during and after each eruption. The vent of the geyser is surprisingly small—about two feet by five feet—and it narrows down to a crack only about four inches wide about 20 feet down. This narrow opening forces the erupting steam and hot water into a high-speed jet. Like a garden hose when you restrict the opening with your thumb, the vent of Old Faithful acts as a nozzle that sprays the column of steam and hot water to its impressive heights.

We recommend at least a two- or three-hour stop at Old Faithful. Go first to the visitor center to get the time estimate of the next eruption, pick up the map of the boardwalk loop trails (up to three miles round-trip), and decide which of the many vents on Geyser Hill you wish to visit. After seeing a couple of the magnificent eruptions of Old Faithful, you may wish to stay for an encore. This place is one of the true natural wonders of the world.

▼ *Below: Boardwalks protect the viewers of the intriguing thermal features in the park. The colorful and interesting geysers, hot springs and mud pots tempt visitors to get an even closer view--but don't do it! Many people have been severely burned and a few killed by these scalding features.*

VOLCANOES ASLEEP

Members of the Washburn Expedition to Yellowstone in 1870 camped overnight in this area, now known as the Upper Geyser Basin. They were so astonished by the beauty of a geyser that they saw in full eruption, and with the regularity of its repeat activity, that they named it "Old Faithful." You can't set your watch by the start of its eruptions, whose show-time intervals have been recorded as short as 30 minutes and as long as 120 minutes, but a little early or a little late, the show does go on. And it has, day and night, summer and winter, for 130 years, and probably for hundreds or thousands of years without anyone but a deer or bison looking up to see it.

The Upper Geyser Basin lies within Yellowstone caldera, but the name "basin" here does not refer to the collapsed caldera. Lava flows that partly fill the caldera—a 115,000 year old flow to the south, and a flow and uplifted dome to the north—form the hills that surround the basin, a much smaller topographic feature than the caldera.

Giantess Geyser on the hill across the Firehole River from Old Faithful erupts even higher than its more faithful sister, with jets to 200 feet that can last for hours. However, if you see it erupting, consider yourself especially lucky. It generally erupts only a few times each year, and is thoroughly unpredictable.

Grand Prismatic Spring, in the Midway Geyser Basin, is nearly 400 feet wide and is the largest hot spring in the United States. It's named for the spectrum of colors of the bacterial mats that rim the steaming pool, and the green and blue light reflected from its clear, deep water. From edge to center, the vivid colors range from brown through orange, red, yellow, and green to, finally, deep blue.

▲ *At Mammoth Hot Springs near the north boundary of the park, terraces of glistening, warm water, rimmed by walls of travertine, form fantastic stone gardens that only nature can create.*

Steamboat Geyser in Yellowstone's Norris Geyser Basin is the world's tallest. Its rare major eruptions, days to decades apart, jet boiling water up to 400 feet high, and on a still day the steam columns can rise even higher. The boiling water phase lasts as long as 20 minutes, followed by a steam eruption whose mighty roar can be heard for miles. In the spring of 2000, it spouted for the first time in nine years to a height of 500 feet.

At Mammoth Hot Springs near the north border of the park, hot, acid water rising through deep fractures dissolve limestone from the layers of marine sediments that were deposited in this region 500 to 200 million years ago. On reaching the surface the hot water cools and precipitates some of its dissolved calcium carbonate into beautiful terraces of travertine. Thermophilic bacteria again produce many of the colors seen in the hot-spring terraces.

The intervals between each of Yellowstone's three giant Yellowstone eruptions lasted close to 650,000 years, and the last great eruption occurred 630,000 years ago. Does that mean another big one will occur during the next 20,000 years? No one knows the answer to that; the regular interval between the huge eruptions may just be coincidental. The time interval between eruptions at many volcanoes is notoriously random and irregular. There have been about 30 smaller volcanic eruptions in Yellowstone since the latest caldera formed 630,000 years ago. That roughly suggests the odds of another one of these smaller eruptions during the next year is about 1 to 20,000, poor odds for an eruption in our lifetimes, but much better than the chance of winning a big lottery.

Many ancient craters from steam explosions are found at Yellowstone. These were apparently caused by the pressure buildup of heated groundwater that was not relieved by the escape valves of geysers or hot springs. The odds of one of these happening during the next year is small, but the number and age of these steam explosion craters are not well enough known to make a numerical estimate of those odds.

Overall, the risk of a volcanic eruption or steam explosion harming a visitor to Yellowstone is too small to worry about. A much greater danger is being scalded by stepping in the wrong place too close to a hot spring or geyser. Stay on the marked trails and boardwalks, and enjoy this grand volcanic park.

▼ *Travertine is calcium carbonate dissolved by hot water from limestone layers at depth, and deposited as solid terrace walls where the water cools. The park's elk are attracted by the warm water.*

Don Pitcher

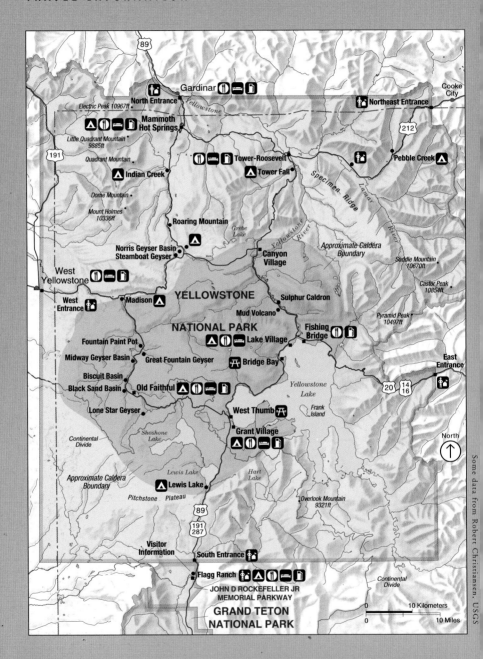

89

Gardinar

Cooke
City

Electric Peak 10967ft

North Entrance

Northeast Entrance

212

Mammoth
Hot Springs

Little Quadrant Mountain
9885ft

191

Quadrant Mountain

Tower-Roosevelt

Pebble Creek

Indian Creek

Tower Fall

Dome Mountain

Specimen Ridge

Mount Holmes
10336ft

Roaring Mountain

Grebe
Lake

Lamar River

Saddle Mountain
10670ft

Norris Geyser Basin
Steamboat Geyser

Approximate Caldera
Boundary

Yellowstone River

Canyon
Village

Castor Peak
10854ft

West
Yellowstone

YELLOWSTONE

Sulphur Caldron

Madison

West
Entrance

NATIONAL PARK

Mud Volcano

Pyramid Peak
10497ft

Fountain Paint Pot

Lake Village

Fishing
Bridge

Midway Geyser Basin

Great Fountain Geyser

Bridge Bay

East
Entrance

Biscuit Basin

Black Sand Basin

Old Faithful

Yellowstone
Lake

20

14
16

Lone Star Geyser

West Thumb

Frank
Island

Continental
Divide

Shoshone
Lake

Grant Village

North

Approximate Caldera
Boundary

Lewis Lake

Lewis Lake

Hart
Lake

Pitchstone   Plateau

Overlook Mountain
9321ft

89

191
287

Visitor
Information

South Entrance

Flagg Ranch

Continental
Divide

JOHN D ROCKEFELLER JR
MEMORIAL PARKWAY

0   10 Kilometers

GRAND TETON
NATIONAL PARK

0   10 Miles

Some data from Robert Christiansen, USGS

▶ GETTING THERE

Yellowstone Park is in northwest Wyoming, 55 miles north of Jackson on US Highway 191; 22 miles west of Cody on US Highway 20; 53 miles south of Livingston, Montana, on US Highway 89; 110 miles southwest of Billings, Montana, on US Highway 212; and 111 miles northeast of Idaho Falls, Idaho, on US Highway 20. There are 370 miles of paved roads within the park. Winter snow will close most of these roads and highways. Nearest airports are at Jackson and Cody, Wyoming; at Idaho Falls and West Yellowstone, Idaho; and at Billings and Bozeman, Montana.

▶ ESSENTIALS

Lodging, camping, food, and gasoline are available at several places within the park. Call the concessionaire (307-344-7311) for lodging and campsite reservations. Other campgrounds open on first-arrival basis. Entrance fees are collected year-round, but many parts of the park are closed in winter.

▶ CLIMATE

Much of Yellowstone is a rolling plateau, nearly 8,000 feet in elevation. Winters are snowy and cold, often below. 0°F. The summer climate is unpredictable; be prepared for most anything from warm sunny days, to thunderstorms, and frost at night.

▶ INFORMATION

Yellowstone National Park
Post Office Box 168
Yellowstone National Park,
Wyoming 82190-0168
Telephone: 307-344-7381
Website: www.nps.gov/yell

▶ VOLCANO FACTS

Name – Yellowstone Volcanic Field
Volcano type – calderas
Rock types – rhyolite and basalt
Height – about 8,000 feet
Oldest dated rocks – 2.2 million years
Latest eruption – 70,000 years ago
    (prehistoric steam explosions from
    heated groundwater are more recent)

Petrified tree stumps on Specimen Ridge were buried by an ancient mudflow and unearthed by erosion

CAPULIN
VOLCANO NATIONAL MONUMENT, NEW MEXICO

Early Spanish explorers called these high plains of northeastern New Mexico "el mar de pasto," the sea of grass. They look much the same today; endless fields of grass and grain. Here and there volcanic hills and peaks break the level of the plains like islands in the sea of grass. Capulin Volcano, a symmetrical cinder cone that rises more than 1,200 feet above the 7,000-foot-high plains is among the youngest and most beautiful of these volcanic vents.

The latest and perhaps only eruption of Capulin Volcano occurred about 60,000 years ago. Although that is just yesterday in geologic time, it is long enough for some volcanoes to be severely eroded. Capulin has maintained its youthful appearance for at least three reasons. First, the lava flows that surround the cone came from "bocas" (Spanish for mouths) at the base of the cinder cone rather than from the crater, a process that preserved the original symmetry of the cone. Also, the climate in this region is dry, which slows down growth of vegetation and soil formation. The cinder cone is also very porous, which allows the rare heavy rains to soak in rather than erode gullies.

We have no eye-witness accounts from 60,000 years ago describing the nature of the basaltic cinder and lava eruptions at Capulin, but luckily, eruptions of some similar cinder cones during the past few decades have been well-studied and described. One of the best examples is Parícutin Volcano in Mexico.

In February 1943, Central Mexico shook from a sharp earthquake, and a long fissure ripped across a farmer's cornfield. From a hole at one end of the crack, steam and bursts of red-hot cinders jetted into the air—the start of a new volcano, later named for the nearby village of Parícutin. That night the new volcano was a dazzling sight, with incandescent bombs hurled as high as 1,500 feet, and lightning flashes bursting through the clouds of steam and ashes. As the fine ashes blew downwind, the coarser fragments of hot but solid lava fell back around the vent, building up a steep cone of cinders. By next morning it was 30 feet high, and by day's end the cinder cone had reached a height of more than 100 feet. During the early months, Parícutin grew remarkably fast. After the first week it

▶ *Opposite: Seen from the north above the western reaches of the Great Plains, Capulin Volcano is easily explored by means of a road that winds to the summit.*

K. Segerstrom, USGS

▲ *The eruption of Capulin Volcano 60,000 years ago was probably similar to the historic eruption of Parícutin Volcano in Mexico from 1943 to 1952. Most of the upward growth of Parícutin's final height of 1,350 feet took place during its first year of eruption. Thick ash-falls seen in this photo destroyed crops, and lava flows issued from vents near the base of the cinder cone.*

was nearly 500 feet high and after ten weeks more than 850 feet. Continuous muffled explosions, one every couple of seconds, lofted steam and ash clouds to 5,000 feet, and hurled hot rock fragments as high as 3,000 feet. The eruption continued in this way for months, with the cone growing in both height and width. Surrounding farms were devastated by the encroaching cone and by thick falls of ash for miles downwind. During this period an occasional lava flow would issue from a boca near the base of the cone, and spread slowly across the surrounding land.

Then, after four months, a new phase of the eruption began. With violent explosions and earthquakes, a crack opened in the side of the crater at the top of the cinder cone, and lava spilled down the side of the mountain. During the next months this flow slowly covered more of the now-abandoned countryside. This was the only time during the entire eruption that lava flowed from the main crater; the large flows to come all issued from bocas.

Later in the year a new crater opened on the side of Parícutin, issuing lava flows and explosions of ash, cinders and bombs. The main crater became less active, erupting mostly steam and ash. As the secondary crater died, a series of new bocas opened on the opposite side of the mountain. These erupted thick, massive flows that slowly engulfed two towns and the village of Parícutin.

The eruption continued with decreasing intensity for the next nine years. The cone had grown to much of its final height of 1,350 feet in the first year. In 1952 the eruption stopped almost as suddenly as it began. Parícutin is now a silent black cone on the plains of central Mexico, a region where there are many prehistoric cinder cones that appear to have erupted during only short periods of activity. It seems probable that the entire life of Parícutin Volcano occurred during the few years between 1943 and 1952.

The similarities of Parícutin and Capulin are striking—high cinder cones surrounded by basaltic lava fields that mainly issued from bocas near their base. However, at Capulin the four main lava flows that cover nearly 16 square miles are mainly pahoehoe flows fed by lava tubes, while at Parícutin the largely block-covered flows are much thicker.

Did Capulin erupt continuously during just a few years, or was it more like Cerro Negro Volcano, a cinder cone in Nicaragua, that has erupted intermittently many times since its birth in the year 1850? It is impossible to reconstruct geologic history with certainty, but by analogy with Parícutin, we favor a short, vigorous life for the eruption and creation of Capulin Volcano. More likely to erupt are new volcanoes in this area, where the record of activity goes back millions of years. Sixty-thousand years is a long sleep, but perhaps not extraordinary for a volcanic area that has already lived eight million years.

Capulin is an easy volcano to explore. There is an old geologist's joke that says there are two types of mountains—those with roads to the top, and those without. The old geologist then adds that he specializes in the former. Capulin would suit him perfectly; it has a

▼ A vent at the base of Cerro Negro Volcano in Nicaragua showers incandescent lumps of molten lava seen in this several-secondtime exposure taken at night in 1968. As the fall-back of lumps of molten lava built this small spatter cone, a slow stream of basaltic lava was also flowing from the vent. While this small but spectacular lower vent eruption was taking place, a thick black cloud of cinders and ash was issuing from the summit crater of Cerro Negro (see photo on page 225).

Andy Parr

paved road that spirals up to a parking lot at the rim of the crater. From there you can hike two trails—a short trail to the bottom of the crater, and a one-mile-long trail around the crater rim. Loose fragments of lava "cinders" cover the edges of both paved trails, and aptly demonstrate why Capulin Volcano is termed a cinder cone.

The views from the rim trail are spectacular. The peak to the southeast is Sierra Grande, the eroded remains of an older volcano rising 2,200 feet above the plains. The majestic mountains to the far west are the Sangre de Cristo Range. Sangre de Cristo means "Blood of Christ" in Spanish, and the mountains were named for their reflected red glow at sunrise and sunset. Low, flat-topped hills rising above the plains are mesas (Spanish for "tables") capped by lavas from older episodes of volcanic activity in this Raton-Clayton volcanic field. Even the name Capulin itself is of Spanish origin; it means "chokecherry," and refers to the small wild fruit trees that grow in the area.

Summer hikers will find wildflowers blooming on Capulin, and sometimes swarms of ladybugs that like to fly up to the crater rim. Adventurous winter hikers (the road may be closed by snow or ice) at this windswept elevation of over 8,000 feet may find the rim trail biting cold.

The visitor center at the base of the volcano has exhibits on the geology, biology, and human history of Capulin. Don't miss the brief video shown in the auditorium telling the story of Capulin's eruption. Outside, the Nature Trail makes for a good, short, informative walk.

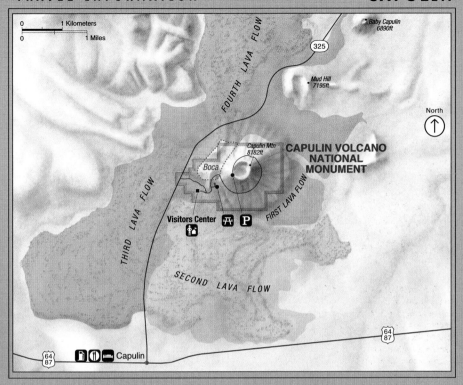

GETTING THERE

Capulin Volcano National Monument is located in northeast New Mexico, 30 miles east of Raton on US Highway 64/87 and three miles north on State Highway 325. Closest commercial airports are in Denver, Colorado, and Albuquerque, New Mexico, each 270 miles away; and in Colorado Springs, Colorado, and Amarillo, Texas, 190 miles away.

ESSENTIALS

The monument is open daily except Thanksgiving, Christmas, and New Year's Day. Volcano Road is closed at night. There is a picnic area near the visitor center, but food, lodging, camping, and gasoline are not available in the monument. Entrance fees are collected year round.

CLIMATE

At an elevation of 7,000 to 8,000 feet, summer temperatures are mild and afternoon thunderstorms are common. Winters are cold and blizzards may close the monument.

INFORMATION

Capulin Volcano National Monument
Post Office Box 40
Capulin, NM 88414
Telephone: 505-278-2201
Website: www.nps.gov/cavo

VOLCANO FACTS

Name – Capulin
Volcano type – cinder cone
    with surrounding lava flows
Rock type – basalt
Height – 1,200 to 1,300 feet above
    surrounding 7,000-foot plains
Last eruption – about 60,000 years ago

EL MALPAIS

El Malpais, the "bad lands." Even to those whose first language is not Spanish, the word has an ominous sound. It was named by explorers from Spain for practical reasons; El Malpais on their map meant a country very difficult to cross on foot and nearly impossible on horseback. These huge areas of rugged lava fields were poured out of volcanoes so young that time has not smoothed them into soil. Imagine walking across 10 miles of large lumps of loose jagged rock as sharp as broken glass, able to destroy a sturdy pair of boots in a day. That's what the surface of an a'a lava flow is like. When exploring such a flow, wear leather gloves and heavy pants in case a fall puts you on your hands and knees.

But the land is not all bad. Its forbidding nature saved the area from development until the time arrived when wilderness became important, not useless. Exploring the fascinating features of El Malpais may be arduous, but is definitely rewarding. It's a time-machine trip to a land that has barely changed since its creation, and by comparing it to volcanic features in Hawaii, we can understand and appreciate its creation.

The best place to start your exploration is the El Malpais Information Center, 23 miles southwest of Grants, New Mexico, on State Highway 53. The monument itself protects a 179-square-mile part of a larger area in northwestern New Mexico known as the Zuni-Bandera volcanic field, a place where lavas poured from the Earth in spasms that began more than half a million years ago. The lava flows in the monument are the youngest outpourings in the Zuni-Bandera field. The McCartys lava flow, the most recent but almost surely not the last, occurred 3,000 years ago.

The McCartys flow is one of the largest young flows in the southwestern United States. It is 36 miles long and two to five miles wide, and its eastern edge forms the boundary of the monument along State Highway 117. The vent of the McCartys flow is a low shield topped by a small cinder cone, and the lava is mainly pahoehoe with patches of a'a. Based on analogies with Hawaiian eruptions, we speculate that the out-

*◀ **Opposite:** Like islands, sandstone mesas jut up through much younger lava flows that cover large areas of west-central New Mexico. Spanish explorers dismissed the arid country as "the bad-lands"–El Malpais.*

*▼ **Below:** During the eruption of cinder cones, large lumps of semi-molten lava called volcanic bombs are often hurled for hundreds of feet into the air. Some volcanic bombs break into fragments when they land; others, like this one, are strong enough to survive their fall.*

Ken Hon, USGS

▲ *Lava tubes, like Big Skylight Cave shown here, are common in the basaltic flows at El Malpais. Sometimes, as seen in this photo, the roof of a cave will collapse in two adjacent places, leaving an arch or bridge of lava spanning the broken cave.*

pouring probably lasted for several years. A fine overview of the flow can be seen from Sandstone Bluffs Overlook, 15 miles south from Interstate 40 (Exit 89) on State Highway 117, near the El Malpais (BLM) Ranger Station.

The eruption of the McCartys flow is still remembered in legend by the Acoma Indians; the Acoma Indian Reservation, with its famous pueblo, lies easterly and adjacent to El Malpais. In their story an evil kachina was blinded by his twin sons so that he could not find the pueblo. The red lava was the blood from the kachina's eyes. After his blood congealed, good finally evolved from evil as ice from drifting winter snows accumulated in the lava-tube caves within the flow. Those ice caves provided a water supply for the Acomas when all other sources dried up.

Ice caves are still a feature of the El Malpais landscape. Bandera Crater and Ice Cave are accessible from a short paved road off State Highway 53, four miles west of the El Malpais Information Center, operated by the park service. These features are on private land, so check at the information center about open hours and fees. Bandera Crater is a large cinder and spatter cone 800 feet high with a 600-foot-deep crater. It erupted about 11,000 years ago and fed flows that extend for 22 miles. The lava-tube caves in these flows have been explored for at least 17 miles, and are the longest known on the North American continent.

Most of El Malpais National Monument is covered by five major lava flows that range in age from 3,000 to 115,000 years. At El Calderon, the 115,000-year-old crater and flow provide vivid evidence of how time begins to subdue even the rugged El Malpais. Enough soil has formed so that groves of aspen and large Douglas fir make the land more hospitable, but its volcanic origin is still unmistakable. The El Calderon parking area lies four miles east of the El Malpais Information Center. The large cinder cone of El Calderon, a mile southwest of the parking area, was created by the fall-back of fragments from high lava fountains that sprayed from the erupting vent. Occasionally large globs of lava as much as three feet across were hurled out, forming lava bombs that can still be found on the slopes of the cone. Molten lava filled the crater and spilled through a breach in the cinder cone to form a flow several miles long. As the fire fountains waned, lava continued to well up on the side of the cone, feeding flows that slowly traveled for more than 20 miles to the northeast. When the El Calderon eruption stopped, molten lava in the crusted-over tubes that fed the flows drained away, leaving behind long, sinuous caves. An entrance to the 3,000-foot-long Junction Cave is just south of the parking lot. Remember that for safe lava-tube cave exploration you need warm clothes, gloves, good boots, a hard hat, and three lanterns or flashlights.

Another one-quarter mile by trail past Junction Cave are the Double Sinks, part of a series of pits and trenches formed by the collapse of a major lava-tube cave in the El Calderon flows. Bat Cave,

▼ *Lost Woman Crater, a forest-covered cinder cone in El Malpais. Five major lava flows in the monument range in age from 115,000 to 3,000 years old. Only the older flows have developed enough soil to support groves of aspen and Douglas fir.*

Ken Hon, USGS

closed to exploration, is a half-mile from the parking area by the same trail. Check at the information center for a ranger-led hike at dusk to see the swarms of bats flying from the cave entrance.

For a true wilderness and historical experience, hike all or part of the rugged eight-mile-long Zuni-Acoma Trail, which crosses El Malpais between State Highways 53 and 117. This foot trail was built a thousand years ago to connect the Acoma and Zuni Indian Pueblos; it crosses a millennium of human history and more than a hundred millennia of geologic history. For safety, let others know your plans and timetable, don't go alone, and take plenty of water.

▼ *The still nearly barren surface of the McCartys lava flow makes it appear even younger than its real 3,000 year age. A much older bluff of sandstone is seen on the right beyond the flow. The McCartys flow is 36-miles long, one of the largest young flows in the southwestern United States.*

Will the Zuni-Bandera volcanic field erupt in the future? Probably; in the past one million years it has undergone approximately 100 eruptions. On average that suggests about one burst of activity every 10,000 years. But "on average" does not mean the interval between eruptive period is always 10,000 years. Four periods of eruption at El Malpais have occurred in the past 17,000 years, with a long period of sleep, about 100,000 years, before that. There might even be a new eruption before the end of the 21st century—but the odds on that are a real long-shot.

Ken Hon, USGS

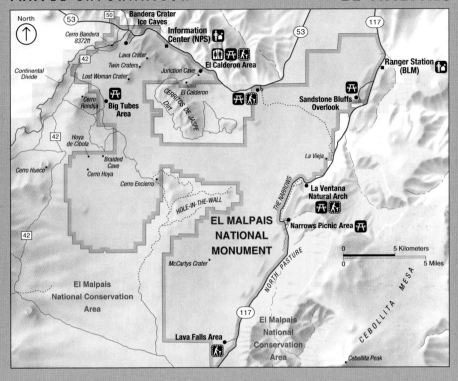

▶ INFORMATION

El Malpais National Monument
123 E. Roosevelt Avenue
Grants, NM 87020
Telephone: 505-285-4641
Website: www.nps.gov/elma

▶ CLIMATE

At elevation ranges from 6,500 to 8,300 feet the weather is unpredictable, so be prepared for all conditions. Thunderstorms are common in summer and snowstorms in winter, but bring sunscreen for plenty of high-altitude sunshine.

▶ GETTING THERE

El Malpais National Monument is located in northwest New Mexico, south of Grants; the Park Service information center is 23 miles south on State Highway 53 from Exit 81 on Interstate 40. The closest major airport is in Albuquerque, New Mexico, 72 miles east.

▶ ESSENTIALS

There are picnic tables, water, and restrooms at the Information Center, but no food, lodging, or gasoline anywhere in the monument. Camping is allowed with a backcountry permit available from the information center, open daily except Thanksgiving, Christmas, and New Year's Day. No entrance fees are charged.

▶ VOLCANO FACTS

Name – Zuni-Bandera Volcanic Field
Volcano types – cinder and spatter cones, lava flows
Rock type – basalt
Heights – cones as high as 800 feet above the surrounding 6,500- to 7,500-foot plains
Latest eruption – about 3,000 years ago

SUNSET CRATER
VOLCANO NATIONAL MONUMENT, ARIZONA

If you tried to think of a state where you could drive in an afternoon through a region dotted with hundreds of volcanoes, Arizona would probably not be the first to come to mind. Yet in northern Arizona, the magnificent San Francisco Volcanic Field covers more than 2,000 square miles, stretching from near Williams to northeast of Flagstaff.

Geologists have found that volcanism in the San Francisco field began near what is now Williams, Arizona. A band of volcanic activity several miles wide has migrated over millions of years toward present-day Flagstaff. The field is named for the spectacular, snow-capped San Francisco Peaks, the highest in Arizona, and remnants of the only stratovolcano in a field of black cinder cones. The highest point of the San Francisco Peaks, Mt. Humphreys, rises to 12,633 feet, but an ancestral mountain was much higher—perhaps 16,000 feet before its summit collapsed sometime between 400,000 and 200,000 years ago. The field contains at least 600 cinder-cone volcanoes—so many, in fact, that only the most prominent, beautiful or unusual have been given names; the rest are known rather ignominiously by number. All the Arizona cinder cones and the jagged lava flows around them look young. In this dry climate there is little erosion, and the lush plant growth that would engulf similar cones in a tropical climate can't get a foothold here.

One of the most beautiful cinder cones—and geologically among the most interesting—has been preserved as Sunset Crater Volcano National Monument. Having started life less than 950 years ago, it is also the youngest volcanic cone (though almost certainly not the last) to grow in this field.

The Sunset Crater eruption began along a fissure about 10 miles long, with lava fountaining along a "curtain of fire" of the type that is common in Hawaii. Eventually the fountains became concentrated in one spot along the fissure, and the cinder cone began to grow from the fallback of cinders and clots of lava from the basaltic lava fountains. Finer ash particles blown by the wind blanketed the countryside, covering more than 800 square miles. Although there are no written descriptions of the eruption by eyewitnesses, there is a Hopi legend of the event. We think this cinder-cone eruption must have been strikingly similar to the eruption of Mexico's Parícutin Volcano, described on pages 212 - 215.

▼ Sunrise at Sunset Crater. The early morning light makes a striking aerial photo of this 600-year-old cinder cone. The youngest of hundreds of volcanic features in northern Arizona, Sunset Crater Volcano erupted while Native Americans were living in the area. Ponderosa pine logs that were used as beams in their buried houses were dated by studying the tree-ring sequences in the wood.

Wendell Duffield, USGS

A nice piece of detective work pins down the year the Sunset Crater eruption began. When scientists working in the area started digging through the ash layers, they discovered remains of many pit-houses buried beneath them, and realized that Native Americans had been living in the area when the eruption began. Ponderosa pine logs that were used as beams in the buried houses were dated by studying their tree-ring sequences, a process called dendrochronology, revealing the time range when the beams were cut. Other studies done on logs that had been stressed but not destroyed by the eruption pinpoint the year even closer, to between the end of the 1064 and the beginning of the 1065 growing seasons.

Most cinder cones have relatively short eruptive histories—a few months or a few years. The duration of activity at Sunset Crater is uncertain; estimates range from years to tens of years. One study even suggests that it may have been active off and on for 130 years— an exceptional age for a cinder cone. Toward the end of its life a large lava flow erupted from the eastern base, and later an even larger one known as the Bonito Flow poured from the western side and ponded in a basin near the cone's base.

The Indians quickly abandoned the area when the eruption started; since no evidence of human remains or valubles have been found in the excavated pit-houses, they must have fled before the worst destruction began. When the eruption stabilized, people began to move back into the area, and communities seemed to flourish. The blanket of volcanic ash not only acted as a mulch to hold soil moisture, but it was rich in minerals valuable for plant growth.

▲ The 1968 eruption of Cerro Negro Volcano, a cinder cone in Nicaragua, is a reasonable analog to the pre-historic eruptions of Capulin and Sunset Crater volcanoes. Notice the red-hot lava fountaining from the lower vent in the foreground (seen close-up in photo on page 215) while a cloud of black ash and cinders erupts from the summit crater. Cerro Negro has been erupting intermittently since 1850, an unusually long life for a cinder cone volcano.

▲ **Above:** Sunset Crater from Bonito Park.

▼ **Below:** Spikes and bloom on a yucca, a common native plant in Arizona.

But eventually the population drifted away again. Geologists feel that the beneficial volcanic ash had finally blown away, so crops declined. Climatologists speculate that weather patterns changed and the climate was too dry for agriculture. Anthropologists point to changing trade networks and agricultural patterns. Astrologers would probably show an inauspicious planetary alignment. In truth, history is a complex web, and a combination of factors were probably at work.

Besides being geologically and historically interesting, Sunset Crater is very beautiful in itself. It is almost perfectly symmetrical— a classic cone, rising 1,000 feet from the surrounding desert. Thanks to the final stages of the eruption, its summit is blanketed with cinders whose oxidized iron content give it a reddish glow, as if bathed in a perpetual sunset. Other minerals like sulfur and gypsum tint some of the cinders inside the crater with purples, yellows and greens.

Sunset Crater was proclaimed a national monument in 1930, but its isolation and poor roads kept visitation low until the 1950s. Travel increased dramatically through the 1970s, and it soon became evident that the footsteps of thousands of people clambering through the soft cinders to reach the summit were causing devastating erosion, so the trail was closed.

Although climbing to the top of the cone is no longer permitted, for a close-up look at volcanic rocks you can hike the Lava Flow Nature Trail on the rough a'a lava of the Bonito Flow, which has been called a "jagged river of stone." It passes old fumaroles, spatter cones, and a cave where ice persists all year. Ice Cave, however, is not open for exploration. Notice the rough, reddish hills in part of the lava flow; these were chunks of the original cone that were torn loose and rafted along in the Bonito Flow. Later phases of the eruption filled in the gaps left in the crater rim, leaving Sunset Crater the almost-perfect cone you see today.

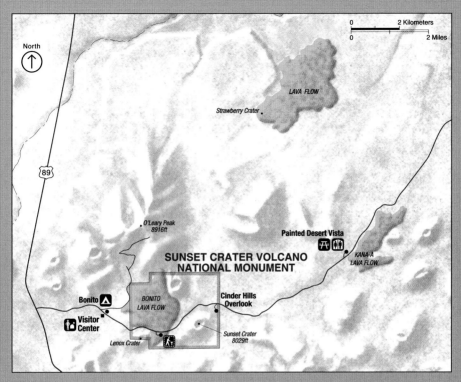

0   2 Kilometers
0   2 Miles

North ↑

LAVA FLOW

Strawberry Crater

89

O'Leary Peak
8916ft

Painted Desert Vista

KANA-A
LAVA FLOW

**SUNSET CRATER VOLCANO
NATIONAL MONUMENT**

Bonito

BONITO
LAVA FLOW

Cinder Hills
Overlook

Visitor
Center

Sunset Crater
8029ft

Lenox Crater

GETTING THERE

Sunset Crater Volcano National Monument is in northern Arizona, 14 miles north of Flagstaff. Take US Highway 89 north for 12 miles and turn right on the road to the monument visitor center. Flagstaff has a commercial airport.

CLIMATE

Elevation ranges from 7,000 to 8,000 feet. Summer days are warm with afternoon thunderstorms possible. Winters are cold with moderate snowfall. Spring and fall have variable weather that can change rapidly.

ESSENTIALS

Entrance fees are collected year round. The visitor center is open every day except Christmas. There are vending machines at the visitor center, but no other food service, lodging, or gasoline available, except for a nearby Forest Service campground (telephone 520-526-0866) and a picnic area in the monument.

INFORMATION

Sunset Crater Volcano National Monument
Route 3, Post Office Box 149
Flagstaff, AZ 86002
Telephone: 520-526-0502
Website: www.nps.gov/sucr

VOLCANO FACTS

Name – Sunset Crater
Volcano type – cinder cone with lava flows
Rock type – basalt
Height – 1,000 to 1,100 feet above the
    surrounding 7,000 foot plateau
Latest eruption – began in AD 1064 or 1065

Part Four

ANCIENT FIRES

Maurice and Katia Krafft, the famous French volcanologists who were killed by a pyroclastic flow from Unzen Volcano in Japan in 1991, once visited us in California. We took them to see Yosemite National Park, but Maurice was not really impressed by the scenery – his passion was erupting volcanoes.

Trying to encourage him into his usual enthusiastic mood, we said, "Look, Maurice, you are right in the middle of an ancient magma chamber." "You are right," he replied, "but I'm a hundred million years too late!"

ANCIENT MAGMA CHAMBERS

From 200 million to 80 million years ago, a subduction zone between the Pacific seafloor and North America existed where the Sierra Nevada now stands. As the ocean floor pushed beneath the continent, magma rose from above the lower plate into huge magma chambers about five miles below the surface of the upper plate. Great chains of stratovolcanoes intermittently fed by these chambers of molten rock stretched along the ancient Sierra. In time the subduction stopped, eventually to be replaced by a side-slipping contact between the plates along the San Andreas fault. The great magma chambers slowly cooled and crystallized into granite, and were uplifted and eroded for millions of years into the bedrock of Yosemite, Sequoia, and Kings Canyon National Parks, and Giant Sequoia National Monument, in California. The volcanoes are gone, mostly eroded away, but the source of their flows can still be seen in the great cliffs and domes of granite carved by glaciers into Yosemite Valley and Kings Canyon.

Three more national parks have somewhat similar geologic origins, but with different timing. The granite massif of 20,320-foot Mt. McKinley, highest peak in North America, is the central theme of Denali National Park, Alaska. As in Yosemite, the granite plutons were once magma chambers created by a major subduction zone between tectonic plates. Here, however, subduction and volcanism began about 100 million years ago and ended some 20 million years ago.

The bedrock geology of North Cascades National Park in Washington is more complex than Yosemite's, but a major part of it is granite of magma-chamber origin. The subduction zone that created it became active about 40 million years ago and still continues today beneath the Cascade volcanoes Mt. Baker and Glacier Peak, which lie west and south of the park, respectively. Some remnants of the older volcanoes can still be found within the park, but most have been eroded away as the mountains rose, exposing their granite cores.

The granite mountains of Acadia National Park on the seacoast of Maine are more gentle and eroded away than Denali, North Cascades, and Yosemite, but are still famous for their beautiful scenery. Here the subduction zone, the vanished volcanoes and their granite roots are much older, generated about 400 to 300 million years ago. The Earth creates beauty at many vast time scales and levels, from soaring Mt. Rainier, built by eruptions on the Earth's surface and still in the making, to the granite core of Denali, melted and tempered deep underground.

▲ **Above:** *Yosemite's Tenaya Lake is surrounded by granite domes that have been sculpted and polished by moving glaciers. The granite cooled from an ancient magma chamber that, when molten, was almost five miles below the Earth's surface. Millions of years of uplift and erosion have exposed its crystallized heart.*

DEADLY ASH

Volcanic ash hurled high into the atmosphere by explosive eruptions falls downwind as a blanket of powdered rock particles. If the layer is a fraction of an inch thick it can be a dusty nuisance. If it falls inches thick, it can kill crops and cause famine. An ashfall only a few feet thick can kill forests and turn waterholes into muddy traps that bury and kill the animals who depend on them. But the plants and animals buried in those ashes may also be preserved. Oxygen and bacteria can be sealed out of their tombs, allowing bones and wood to be petrified by the abundant silica in the ash. These preserved fossils are a bonanza to paleontologists, who use them to date the deposits in which they occur, and to establish the links in the process of the evolution of life.

John Day Fossil Beds National Monument, Oregon, is one of the best places on Earth for finding fossil plants and animals. The ages of the fresh-water sediments and volcanic ashfalls provide an almost-continuous record of the flora and fauna that lived here from 54 to

▲ Called the "stone wind" by the few survivors near the edge of the great blast of expanding gas and ash from the initial explosion of Mount St. Helens in 1980, this hot, dense, high-velocity cloud destroyed 230 square miles of forest land in Washington (see pages 64-75).

6 million years ago. Some of the death and preservation was due to volcanoes, and the dates that can be established from volcanic rocks interlayered with the sediments provide a timetable for the fossil record. That record is remarkable for its diversity—tropical forests change to temperate grasslands, horses evolve from the early specimens the size of small dogs, and many strange mammals, including an ancestral elephant, appear and disappear in North America.

Florissant Fossil Beds National Monument in Colorado is another trove of buried insects and plants that have been preserved by volcanic ash. Thirty-four million years ago the area contained a long lake surrounded by forests that included redwoods, cedars, maples, and oaks. Then, nearby volcanic eruptions filled the air with ash. Insects and leaves fell into the lake and were buried and fossilized within the fine ash layers. More than 60,000 specimens have been collected for museums around the world, including many so well preserved that 1,100 insect species have been identified. Some butterfly species still exist today, but tsetse flies found in the ancient ash layers have fortunately disappeared from North America. Volcanic mudflows also buried and petrified stumps and logs from the forests that surrounded the lake.

Nowhere can the beauty of petrified wood be seen better than in Petrified Forest National Park in Arizona. Two hundred million years ago this area, now known as the Painted Desert, was a flood plain and delta accumulating silty sediments that were eroded from a higher region to the south. Volcanoes in that region also provided many ash layers to the thickening sedimentary layers. Logs of ancient conifer trees, possibly downed by volcanic activity as the forests around Mount St. Helens were destroyed by its 1980 eruption, were carried down the rivers and buried in the flood-plain sediments. Over

▼ *The fossil wasp (bottom left), fruit of the Golden Rain Tree (bottom right), and Robber Fly (immediately below) were preserved in fine volcanic ash layers in an ancient lake at what is now Florissant Fossil Beds National Monument, Colorado. Volcanoes in this area 34 million years ago filled the air with ash. Insects that fell into the lake were buried and preserved in the ash that settled to the lake bottom. Uplift and erosion have exposed the old lake sediments.*

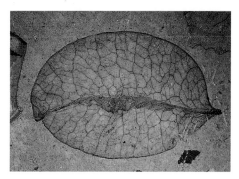

Owen Callahan, NPS

DEADLY ASH

233

▲ **Above:** *A broken stone log at Petrified Forest National Park in Arizona. Trees swept by ancient rivers into flood plain and delta sediments about 200 million years ago were buried by silt and mud containing volcanic ash. It is not clear that the trees were killed by volcanic eruptions, but the abundant silica in the ash-laden mud helped convert the buried wood to agate and other colorful silica minerals.*

▼ **Below:** *This tree stump was petrified in place at Florissant Fossil Beds National Monument.*

the eons that followed, underground water laden with silica that had been leached from the volcanic ash layers, slowly turned the giant logs into stone. Red, yellow, brown, and creamy white agate replaced the wood, but in many places preserved its original grain, making entire logs into hard semi-precious gemstone. Uplift and erosion of the Colorado Plateau in the past few million years has returned many of the logs of the Petrified Forest back to the Earth's surface. Many petrified wood specimens erode from the red, brown, and white layers of the Painted Desert outside the park, so it is legally possible for collectors to find or buy beautiful chunks of petrified wood.

Other fossils that may or may not be related to volcanic ashfalls are the beautifully preserved specimens of fossil fish from the sediments in ancient lakes of southwestern Wyoming. Fossil Butte National Monument was established to protect part of this unusual occurrence of plant, animal, and especially fish fossils preserved in the 50-million-year old bottom sediments of long-gone Fossil Lake. Millions of fish perished and were buried in a layer of shale about a foot thick. Was this some catastrophic event, or was the bottom water of the lake so toxic that fish swimming into it died and their remains were not eaten by scavengers? Volcanic ash beds are present along with the silts and clays of the lake sediments, but their possible role in the fish-kills remains a mystery.

Robert Krimmel, USGS

The classic view of the occurrence of most land-animal fossils is that drought, predators, accidents, or old age killed the animals in certain places where their bones were buried and preserved by flood-plain sediments. This is the conventional story at Hagerman Fossil Beds in Idaho, Badlands National Park in South Dakota, Theodore Roosevelt National Park in North Dakota, Agate Fossil Beds in Nebraska, and Dinosaur National Monument in Utah. Perhaps it is just coincidence that volcanic ash—some whose source may have been hundreds to thousands of miles away—occurs at all these places mixed in with the flood-plain formations that contain the fossils. The Ashfall Fossil Beds State Historical Park in Nebraska preserves a recent find of hundreds of horses, camels, birds, and even a mother rhinoceros and her baby, in a foot-thick volcanic ash layer that destroyed their water hole. The source of that ash layer has been identified from a 12 million year old eruption of the Yellowstone Hot Spot.

Not all volcanic ash eruptions are deadly; most of the smaller ones are not. In fact, volcanic ash helps to create life, not destroy it. The powdered rock particles that make up volcanic ash contain both potassium and phosphorous minerals, and as chemical weathering from rain slowly breaks down these minerals, soluble molecules of potassium and phosphorous—essential plant nutrients—become available. In effect it is Nature's slow-release fertilizer. It has long been known that soils in active volcanic regions are exceedingly fertile.

▲ The May 1980 eruption of Mount St. Helens Volcano rudely reminded us all that volcanoes can be beasts as well as beauties. The huge explosion, triggered by one of the largest landslides in recorded history, killed 57 people. The summit of Mount St. Helens was reduced from 9,677 feet to 8,365 feet in just a few violent minutes. Ash jetted into the sky for several hours following the initial explosion. (See pages 64-75.)

HOODOOS & HOMESITES

▲ Hoodoos eroded from thick pyroclastic-flow deposits in Arizona's Chiricahua National Monument, a wild country once home to Geronimo, the Apache Indian warrior. The thousands of fantastic spires and balanced rocks are the eroded remains of the Rhyolite Canyon Tuff that surged across 1,200 square miles of land here, 27 million years ago. A great caldera, 12 miles across and a thousand feet deep, was created by the eruption, but has been largely obscured by later mountain building and erosion.

Hoodoo really is a geological term; it is defined as a fantastic column or pillar of rock. A land of hoodoos perfectly describes the fantastic, unusual, yet beautiful landscape of Chiricahua National Monument in Arizona. The Rhyolite Canyon Tuff, the bedrock of the monument, was violently erupted from a volcano a few miles to the south. As the massive pyroclastic flow that deposited the welded tuff surged across an area of more than 1,200 square miles, a huge caldera 12 miles across sank nearly a mile into the partly emptied magma chamber. All this occurred about 27 million years ago, enough time for basin-and-range faulting and erosion to have obscured the shape of the great caldera. Vertical cracks that formed as the welded tuff cooled were the first stage in the creation of the hoodoos; rain, chemical weathering, wind, and gravity over time have enlarged the fractures into the legions of fantastic columns you see there today.

Other ancient calderas are common in southern Arizona, and two more of them are in national parks. Saguaro National Park, near Tucson, is a desert region famous for its giant cacti, but the complex geology of its western section is interesting as well. The 73-million-year-old Tucson Mountains caldera has been tilted, broken by basin and range faulting, and so severely eroded that its 12- by 15-mile basin is only discernible by careful geologic mapping. Much of the bedrock

ANCIENT FIRES

of the area is the Cat Mountain tuff that was erupted during the caldera-collapse eruption. The Ajo Mountains in the eastern part of Organ Pipe Cactus National Monument, just north of the Mexican border, are largely composed of gently tilted layers of volcanic rocks that include rhyolitic tuffs erupted some 20 million years ago.

The volcano that created Pinnacles National Monument in California about 23 million years ago erupted some thick, viscous rhyolite lava flows and also disgorged huge volumes of pyroclastic flows. The tuff deposits from these fiery flows of hot gases and rock fragments welded into thick, massive formations. These cooled and contracted, breaking into thousands of vertical cracks that have since eroded into the myriad pinnacles for which the monument is named. The Pinnacles volcano is also geologically famous for another reason. When active, it grew on top of the San Andreas fault; as the fault intermittently jerked sideways over millions of years it split the volcano in two. The largest part is now Pinnacles, and the other part is now nearly 200 miles south near Lancaster, California, and is called the Neenach Formation.

The caldera collapse that created the 13-mile-wide Valle Grande near Santa Fe, New Mexico, occurred just over a million years ago, so the shape and beauty of this huge caldera is still well-preserved. More well known is the plateau-like apron of pyroclastic-flow deposits, the Bandelier Tuff, that spewed out of Valle Grande. This high, remote plateau is the site of Los Alamos, the town where the atomic bomb was invented. Nearby, in a deep canyon eroded into the compact but fairly soft tuff, is Bandelier National Monument, a 13th century Indian Pueblo whose ruins include many rooms that were cut into the near-vertical cliffs.

▲ **Above and below:** *Los Alamos, New Mexico, the birthplace of the atomic bomb, lies on a high mesa of thick pyroclastic-flow deposits called the Bandelier Tuff, erupted about a million years ago. A thousand years ago, ancient Pueblo builders carved cliff dwellings into the soft but durable walls of canyons eroded into the tuff. Seen here are the ruins of a Pueblo settlement in Bandelier National Monument, adjacent to Los Alamos.*

BEDROCK LAVA

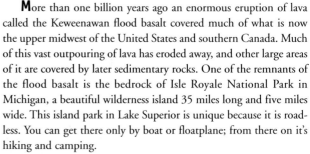

▼ Early Hawaiians carved
many thousands of petro-
glyphs into the smooth
surface of pahoehoe lava
flows. Pictured here is a
Hawaiian canoe with its dis-
tinctive curved sail *(upper)*
and a stylized turtle.

More than one billion years ago an enormous eruption of lava called the Keweenawan flood basalt covered much of what is now the upper midwest of the United States and southern Canada. Much of this vast outpouring of lava has eroded away, and other large areas of it are covered by later sedimentary rocks. One of the remnants of the flood basalt is the bedrock of Isle Royale National Park in Michigan, a beautiful wilderness island 35 miles long and five miles wide. This island park in Lake Superior is unique because it is road-less. You can get there only by boat or floatplane; from there on it's hiking and camping.

The Keweenaw National Historic Park on the Upper Peninsula of Michigan is also underlain by the ancient flood basalt. Here the lava contains pieces of native cop-per—metallic copper that does not have to be smelted. Native Americans used this unusual source of copper for thousands of years, and rich mines were later developed here to supply copper for the industrial revolution.

Most of the islands of the world that rise from the deep ocean basins are of volcanic origin. Even coral atolls are mainly a cap of limestone on top of a lava foundation. The bedrock of the Hawaiian and Samoan islands is basalt; without volcanism the islands would not exist. All the national parks there, including the National Park of American Samoa, a mountainous rainforest and a coral reef, owe their very existence to bedrock lava. In addition to the two Hawaiian nationals parks already mentioned—Hawaii Volcanoes (pages 52-63) and Haleakala (pages 126-133)—three Hawaiian national monuments preserve examples of bedrock lava. Kalaupapa National Historical Park, site of a leper colony in Hawaii established in 19th century is located on a small, isolated, volcanic peninsula on the north side of Molokai. Pu'u Honua O Honaunau

J.D. Griggs, USGS

National Historic Park (often called "City of Refuge"), on the Kona coast of the Big Island, provided refuge from punishment for ancient Hawaiians who could get within its massive walls before being caught by their pursuers. Pu'ukohola Heiau National Historic Site, a huge temple built of lava blocks on the west coast of the Big Island, was founded on command of Kamehameha I, the chief who united the main Hawaiian Islands by conquest.

Beyond creating islands, landscapes, and shelter, an ancient volcano near Albuquerque, New Mexico, provided a unique product. At Petroglyph National Monument, Native Americans supplied the art, but a 130,000 year-old lava flow supplied the "canvas." Thousands of drawings were chipped into the flat surfaces of basalt outcrops and boulders on the west side of the Rio Grande River.

▲ **Above:** *New bedrock being added to Hawaii. Lava from Kilauea Volcano flows in lava tubes for many miles down the mountain's flanks to the sea. In this photo a bench of hardened lava has broken off and fallen into the ocean, exposing the end of a live lava tube.*

STILL OTHERS

Devils Tower National Monument in Eastern Wyoming is a prominent, steep-sided landmark 1,250 feet high. The impressive structures of this volcanic feature are the vertical columnar joints that resulted from its cooling at shallow depth. Although that depth has been estimated to be only 1,000 to 3,000 feet below the surface when the intruded rock cooled some 40 million years ago, there is no remaining evidence that any lava flowed on the surface. The argument, then, is whether Devils Tower was a volcanic neck—the feeder conduit to a volcano—or a shallow intrusion of magma that domed up into the overlying sedimentary layers, but did not erupt. If it was not a true volcano, it was close.

Finally, we end with the volcanoes that dammed the Colorado River and, for a while, created huge reservoirs in what is now Grand Canyon National Park in Arizona. During the past two million years, volcanoes mainly on the north side of the western region of the canyon spilled large basaltic lava flows down into the river channel at least thirteen times, the latest about 400,000 years ago. These lava dams filled the canyon for many miles downstream, and the largest one reached a height of 2,300 feet above the present river level. Below Canyon Village in the park, the impounded lake was about 1,600 feet deep. As the reservoir that backed up behind this huge plug of lava began to overflow the top of the dam, a great waterfall eroded its way upstream until the original channel was restored. The estimate for the time it took to fill the largest lake is several years; the estimates for its draining range from hundreds to thousands of years. The future will probably bring new reservoirs into Grand Canyon. Let's be patient; Nature can certainly do the job, and repair it, better than humans can.

◄ *Overleaf:*
A line of lava fountains 50– to 75–feet high create a "curtain of fire" during the eruption of Mauna Loa in 1984. The eruption began high on the Northeast Rift Zone of the volcano. Flows extended many miles down the mountain toward the city of Hilo (see photo on page 60). The dark gray flow on which the geologists are standing is older, solidified lava, but the silvery gray flow at the base of the fountains is hot, molten rock.
Dick Moore, USGS

◄ *Opposite:*
Devils Tower, a 1,250-foot-high landmark in Devils Tower National Monument, Wyoming, is an igneous rock feature that intruded into sedimentary rock layers about 40 million years ago. Older interpretations considered the structure to be a volcanic neck–the feeder conduit to a surface volcano now eroded away. More recent studies conclude that the molten rock cooled at a depth of 1,000 to 3,000 feet and never reached the ancient land surface–an "almost" volcano.

RECOMMENDED BOOKS & WEBSITES

GENERAL REFERENCES

Brock, T.D., *Life at High Temperatures.* Yellowstone Association, 1994.

Bryan, T.S., *The Geysers of Yellowstone,* third edition. University Press of Colorado, 1995.

Decker, Robert, and Barbara Decker, *Volcanoes,* third edition. W.H. Freeman and Company, 1998.

Duffield, Wendell A., *Volcanoes of Northern Arizona.* Grand Canyon Association, 1997.

Fisher, Richard V., Grant Heiken, and J.B. Hulen, *Volcanoes: Crucibles of Change.* Princeton University Press, 1997.

Harris, D.V., and E.P. Kiver, *The Geologic Story of the National Parks and Monuments,* fourth edition. John Wiley and Sons, 1985.

Kious, W.J., and Robert I. Tilling, *This Dynamic Earth: the Story of Plate Tectonics.* U.S. Geological Survey, 1996.

Moores, E.M. ed., *Shaping the Earth: Tectonics of Continents and Oceans.* W.H. Freeman and Company, 1990.

Simkin, Tom, and Lee Siebert, *Volcanoes of the World,* second edition. Smithsonian Institution, 1994.

Simkin, Tom, John D. Unger, Robert I. Tilling, Peter R. Vogt, and Henry Spall, *This Dynamic Planet: World Map of Volcanoes, Earthquakes, Impact Craters, and Plate Tectonics.* U.S. Geological Survey, 1994.

Sullivan, Walter, *Continents in Motion.* McGraw-Hill Book Company, 1991.

Wood, Charles A., and Juergen Kienle, *Volcanoes of North America.* Cambridge University Press, 1990.

Dartmouth's Electronic Volcano: www.dartmouth.edu/~volcano/

Michigan Technological University Volcanoes Page: www.geo.mtu.edu/volcanoes

National Park Service (Park Net): www.nps.gov/parks.html

Park Geology Tour of Hot Springs: www2.nature.nps.gov/grd/tour/hotsprin.htm

Park Geology Tours: www2.nature.nps.gov/grd/tour/index.htm

Smithsonian Institution Global Volcanism Program: www.volcano.si.edu/gvp

U.S. Geological Survey Volcano Hazards Program: volcanoes.usgs.gov

University of North Dakota Volcano World: volcano.und.nodak.edu

Volcanoes Online: library.thinkquest.org/17457

PARK REFERENCES

ANIAKCHAK NATIONAL MONUMENT, ALASKA

Alaska Geographic, *Alaska's Volcanoes.* Alaska Geographic Society, 1991

Bodeau, J., *Katmai National Park.* Alaska Natural History Association, 1995.
(Includes Aniakchak)

Alaska Volcano Observatory: www.avo.alaska.edu
(go to "ATLAS"; then go to alphabetical list)

Park Geology: www2.nature.nps.gov/grd/parks/ania/index.htm

CAPULIN VOLCANO NATIONAL MONUMENT, NEW MEXICO

Parent, Laurence, James McCristal, and Allyson Mathis,
Capulin Volcanic National Monument.
Southwest Parks and Monuments Association, 1999.

Capulin Volcanic Park Geology: www.aqd.nps.gov/grd/parks/cavo/index.htm

University of North Dakota Volcano World: volcano.und.nodak.edu
(type "Capulin" in Search Box)

CRATER LAKE NATIONAL PARK, OREGON

Decker, Robert, and Barbara Decker,
Road Guide to Crater Lake National Park
Double Decker Press, 1995.

Nelson, C.H., Charles R. Bacon, and others,
"The volcanic, sedimentologic, and paleolimnologic history of the Crater Lake
caldera floor, Oregon." Geological Society of America, v. 106, pp.684-704, 1994.

Schaffer, Jeffrey P., *Crater Lake National Park and Vicinity.* Wilderness Press, 1983

Cascades Volcano Observatory: vulcan.wr.usgs.gov/Volcanoes/CraterLake

Crater Lake Park Geology: www2.nature.nps.gov/grd/parks/crla

CRATERS OF THE MOON NATIONAL MONUMENT, IDAHO

National Park Service, Handbook 139,
Craters of the Moon. National Park Service, 1991

Cascade Volcano Observatory:
vulcan.wr.usgs.gov/Volcanoes/Idaho/CratersMoon/

Craters of the Moon Park Geology:
www2.nature.nps.gov/grd/parks/crmo/index.htm

DEATH VALLEY NATIONAL PARK, CALIFORNIA

Decker, Barbara, and Robert Decker, *Road Guide To Death Valley.*
Double Decker Press, 1999.

Sharp, Robert P., and Alan F. Glazner, *Geology Underfoot In Death Valley And Owens Valley.* Mountain Press, 1997.

Death Valley Park Geology: www.aqd.nps.gov/grd/parks/deva/index.htm

University of North Dakota Volcano World: volcano.und.nodak.edu
(type "Ubehebe" in Search Box)

DEVILS POSTPILE NATIONAL MONUMENT, CALIFORNIA

Huber, N. King, and Wymond W. Eckhardt,
Devils Postpile Story. Sequoia Natural History Association, 1985.

Long Valley Observatory:
quake.wr.usgs.gov/VOLCANOES/LongValley/index.html

Devils Postpile Park Geology: wrgis.wr.usgs.gov/docs/parks/depo/dpgeol1.html

EL MALPAIS NATIONAL MONUMENT, NEW MEXICO

Mabery, Marilyn B.(Ed.), Richard B. Moore, and Ken A. Hon,
The Volcanic Eruptions of El Malpais. Ancient City Press, 1999.

El Malpais Park Geology: www2.nature.nps.gov/grd/parks/elma

Southwest Parks Information:
www.swparks.com/us/travel/newmexico/elmalpais.html

HALEAKALA NATIONAL PARK, HAWAII

Decker, Barbara, and Robert Decker,
Road Guide to Haleakala and the Hana Highway.
Double Decker Press, 1999.

Macdonald, Gordon A., Agatin Abbot, and Frank Peterson,
Volcanoes in the Sea, second edition. University of Hawaii Press, 1995.

Haleakala Park Geology: www2.nature.nps.gov/grd/parks/hale/

Hawaiian Volcano Observatory: hvo.wr.usgs.gov/volcanoes/haleakala/

HAWAII VOLCANOES NATIONAL PARK, HAWAII

Decker, Barbara, and Robert Decker,
Road Guide to Hawaii Volcanoes National Park.
Double Decker Press, 1997.

Hazlett, Richard W., and Donald W. Hyndman,
Roadside Geology of Hawaii., Mountain Press, 1996.

Big Island Virtual Field Trips: mael.soest.hawaii.edu/space/hawaii/all.bi.vfts.html

Hawaiian Volcano Observatory: hvo.wr.usgs.gov

Hawaii Volcanoes Park Geology: www2.nature.nps.gov/grd/parks/havo/index.htm

KATMAI NATIONAL PARK AND PRESERVE, ALASKA

Alaska Geographic Society, *Katmai Country*. Alaska Geographic Society, 1989.

Bodeau, J., *Katmai National Park*. Alaska Natural History Association, 1995.

Hildreth, Wes, and Judy Fierstein,
"The Katmai Volcanic Cluster and the Great Eruption of 1912."
Bulletin of the Geological Society of America, v. 112, n. 10, p. 1594-1620, 2000.

National Geographic Magazine
articles on Katmai in February 1913, January 1917, February 1918, and
September 1921.

Alaska Volcano Observatory: www.avo.alaska.edu
(go to "ATLAS"; then go to alphabetical list)

Katmai Park Geology: www.nature.nps.gov/grd/parks/katm/index.htm

LAKE CLARK NATIONAL PARK AND PRESERVE, ALASKA

Belous, R. (Ed.),
The Sierra Club Guides to the National Parks of the Northwest and Alaska.
Random House, 1996.

Brantley, Steven R., *The Eruption of Redoubt Volcano, Alaska,
1989-1990.* U.S. Geological Survey, Circular 1061, 1990.

Alaska Volcano Observatory: www.avo.alaska.edu
(go to "ATLAS"; then go to alphabetical list)

U.S. Geological Survey Volcano Hazards Program: volcanoes.usgs.gov

LASSEN VOLCANIC NATIONAL PARK, CALIFORNIA

Decker, Robert, and Barbara Decker,
Road Guide to Lassen Volcanic National Park.
Double Decker Press, 1997.

Schaffer, Jeffrey P., *Lassen Volcanic National Park and Vicinity.*
Wilderness Press, 1981.

Cascades Volcano Observatory: vulcan.wr.usgs.gov

Lassen Park Geology: www2.nature.nps.gov/grd/parks/lavo/index.htm

U.S. Geological Survey Volcano Hazards Program: volcanoes.usgs.gov

LAVA BEDS NATIONAL MONUMENT, CALIFORNIA

Donnelly-Nolan, Julie M., and D.E. Champion,
Geologic Map of Lava Beds National Monument, Northern California.
U.S. Geological Survey Map I-1804, 1987.

Donnelly-Nolan, Julie,
Medicine Lake Volcano and Lava Beds National Monument, California.
Geological Society of America Centennial Field Guide #66, 1987.

Cascade Volcano Observatory: vulcan.wr.usgs.gov/Volcanoes/MedicineLake/

University of North Dakota Volcano World: volcano.und.nodak.edu
(type "Medicine Lake" in Search Box)

MOJAVE NATIONAL PRESERVE, CALIFORNIA

Sharp, Robert P., and Alan F. Glazner,
Geology Underfoot in Southern California.
Mountain Press, 1993.

Wood, Charles A., and Juergen Kienle,
Volcanoes of North America.
Cambridge University Press, 1990.

Mojave Park Geology: www2.nature.nps.gov/grd/parks/moja/index.htm

U. S. Geological Survey Park Geology:
www2.nature.nps.gov/grd/usgsnps/mojave/mojave1.html

MOUNT RAINIER NATIONAL PARK, WASHINGTON

Decker, Barbara, and Robert Decker,
Road Guide to Mount Rainier National Park.
Double Decker Press, 1996.

Harris, Stephen L.,
Fire Mountains of the West.
Mountain Press Publishing Co., 1988.

Cascades Volcano Observatory: vulcan.wr.usgs.gov/Volcanoes/Rainier/

Mt. Ranier Park Geology: www2.nature.nps.gov/grd/parks/mora

MOUNT ST. HELENS
NATIONAL VOLCANIC MONUMENT, WASHINGTON

Carson, Rob, *Mount St. Helens.* Sasquatch Books, 1999.

Decker, Robert, and Barbara Decker,
Road Guide to Mount St. Helens.
Double Decker Press, 1993.

Cascades Volcano Observatory: vulcan.wr.usgs.gov

U.S. Geological Survey Volcano Hazards Program: volcanoes.usgs.gov

NEWBERRY NATIONAL VOLCANIC MONUMENT, OREGON

Jensen, Robert A.,
Roadside Guide to the Geology of Newberry Volcano,
second edition. 1995.

Newberry National Volcanic Monument:
www.fs.fed.us/r6/deschutes/monument/monument.html

University of North Dakota Volcano World:
volcano.und.nodak.edu (type "Newberry" in Search Box)

SUNSET CRATER VOLCANO NATIONAL MONUMENT, ARIZONA

Duffield, Wendell A.,
Volcanoes of Northern Arizona.
Grand Canyon Association, 1997.

Sunset Crater Park Geology:
www2.nature.nps.gov/grd/usgsnps/sunset/sunset1.html

WRANGELL-ST. ELIAS NATIONAL PARK AND PRESERVE, ALASKA

Belous, R., ed.,
The Sierra Club Guides to the National Parks of the Northwest and Alaska.
Random House, 1996.

National Park Service, and Alaska Natural History Association,
A Geologic Guide to Wrangell-St. Elias National Park and Preserve, Alaska
U.S. Geological Survey, Professional Paper 1616, 2000

Richter, Donald H., D.S. Rosenkrans, and M.J. Steigerwald,
Guide to the Volcanoes of the Western Wrangell Mountains, Alaska.
U.S. Geological Survey, 1995.

Alaska Volcano Observatory: www.avo.alaska.edu
(go to "ATLAS"; then go to alphabetical list)

U.S. Geological Survey Volcano Hazards Program: volcanoes.usgs.gov

YELLOWSTONE NATIONAL PARK, WYOMING, MONTANA, AND IDAHO

Brock, T.D., *Life at High Temperatures.*
Yellowstone Association, 1994.

Bryan, T.S.,
The Geysers of Yellowstone,
Third Edition. University Press of Colorado, 1995.

Christiansen, Robert L.,
*The Quaternary and Pliocene Yellowstone Plateau Volcanic Field
of Wyoming, Idaho, and Montana.*
U.S. Geological Survey Professional Paper 729-G, in press.

Smith, Robert B., and Lee J. Siegel,
*Windows into the Earth: The Geologic Story of Yellowstone
and Grand Teton National Parks.*
Oxford University Press, 2000.

Cascade Volcano Observatory: vulcan.wr.usgs.gov/Volcanoes/Yellowstone/

Robert Smith Home Page: www.mines.utah.edu/~rbsmith/rbs-home.index.html

Yellowstone National Park: www.nps.gov/yell/

Yellowstone Park Geology: www2.nature.nps.gov/grd/parks/yell/index.htm

ACKNOWLEDGMENTS

We are always amazed at the generosity with which people contribute their information, expertise, photographs, and time to a project like this. We are grateful to our friends from the U.S. Geological Survey, the National Park Service, and other institutions who have generously helped us with this book. We especially want to thank Tina Neal, Dallas Peck, Bob Tilling, Judy Fierstein, Wes Hildreth, Game McGimsey, Don Richter, Joe McGregor, Jane Takahashi, Don Peterson, Jim Griggs, David Little, David Wieprecht, Ron Warfield, Tom Sisson, Dwight Hamilton, Jim Quiring, Don Reeser, Roger Henneberger, John Kjargaard, Dave Sherrod, Charlie Bacon, Mike Clynne, Bob Christiansen, Patrick Muffler, Scott Isaacson, Nancy Bailey, Steve Brantley, Lyn Topinka, Mike Doukas, Bob Jensen, Julie Donnelly-Nolan, King Huber, Jim Moore, Roy Bailey, Ralph Klinger, Rick Hazlett, Joan DeGraff, Andy Leszcykowski, Bill Bonnichsen, Doug Owen, Bob Smith, Allyson Mathis, Jane Kwak, Dick Moore, Ken Hon, Wendell Duffield, Ed du Bray, Peter Stauffer, Sue Mayfield, Peter Lipman, Keith Ronnholm, Chuck O'Rear, Herb Meyer, Ruth Ann Warden, Dave Clark and Rick Frost.

Our thanks also to Chris Burt of Compass American Guides who first put us on this quest and to Magnus Bartlett, Publisher, who trusted us to write this book. And of course we thank Barry Parr, Editor, and Leslie Wilks, Designer, for working tirelessly to put all the parts together.

GLOSSARY

a'a
A type of lava flow having a rough, jagged surface.

accreted terranes
A geographical area composed of segments of land transported from other regions by tectonic movement along faultlines.

active volcano
A volcano that is currently erupting, or has erupted in recorded history.

aerosol
A suspension of fine liquid or solid particles in air.

airfall deposit
Volcanic debris that has fallen from an eruption cloud.

andesite
A gray volcanic rock common to stratovolcanoes, with a silica content between basalt and dacite.

angle of repose
The steepest slope at which loose material will come to rest without slumping.

ash cloud
A cloud of ash formed by a volcanic eruption.

ash, volcanic
Fine fragments of lava or rock, down to dust size, formed by volcanic explosions.

ashfall
Volcanic ash falling from an eruption column or ash cloud.

avalanche
A large mass of earth, rock, volcanic debris, etc., descending swiftly down a mountain.

basalt
Dark-colored lava rich in iron and magnesium, containing about 50 percent silica.

block, volcanic
A solid fragment of lava or rock thrown out in an explosive eruption; larger than two inches in size.

bomb, volcanic
A lump of lava thrown out of a volcano while still molten; takes on a rounded shape.

caldera
A large basin-shaped depression at a volcano's summit, usually formed by collapse.

cinder cone
A steep hill formed by the accumulation around a vent of cinders and other fragments expelled in an eruption.

cinder, volcanic
A lava fragment of about 1/2 inch in diameter.

complex volcano
A volcano with two or more summits in close proximity.

composite volcano
See *stratovolcano*.

conduit
The crack or tube through which magma moves.

continental crust
The solid outer layers of the Earth beneath continents; less dense and thicker than oceanic crust. Normally about 15 miles in thickness.

continental drift
The theory that continents slowly move their positions relative to one another on the Earth's surface.

convergent margin
The seam between two converging tectonic plates.

crater
A bowl- or funnel-shaped depression; often a major vent of volcanic products.

crater row
A line of craters built by a fountaining lava eruptions that take place along a fissure.

crystalline rock
A rock composed of interlocking crystals.

curtain of fire
A line of lava fountains erupting along a fissure.

dacite
A light-colored volcanic rock, intermediate in silica composition between rhyolite and andesite.

dike
A blade-shaped body of intrusive igneous rock that cuts across the layering of the country rock.

directed blast
A hot mixture of rock debris, ash, and gases, generated by a volcanic explosion, that is propelled horizontally away from the vent at a high speed.

divergent margin
The tear where two tectonic plates that are moving apart.

dormant volcano
A volcano that is not currently erupting but is considered likely to do so in the future.

eruption cloud
A cloud of gas, ash, and other fragments generated by a volcanic eruption.

explosive eruption
A sudden expansion of gases laden with volcanic fragments; caused by explosive boiling.

extinct volcano
A volcano that is not expected to erupt again; a dead volcano.

fault
A fracture in the Earth's crust along which there has been movement.

fault scarp
A steep slope or cliff formed by movement along a fault.

feldspar
A light-colored mineral composed largely of oxygen, silicon, and aluminum.

fissure
A large, blade-shaped crack in the Earth.

fumarole
An opening in the ground from which volcanic gases and steam are emitted.

fume cloud
A gaseous cloud without volcanic ash.

geophysics
The physical and mechanical aspects of geology.

granite
A coarse-grained igneous rock composed mostly of quartz and feldspar.

hot-spot volcanoes
Volcanoes related to a persistent heat source in the mantle.

hydrothermal alteration
The breakdown of volcanic rocks by the action of percolating hot water.

igneous rock
Magma or lava that has cooled and solidified below or above ground.

intrusion
A rock body formed by magma forcing its way into surrounding host rock and then cooling; also the process of forming such a rock body.

lava
Magma that has reached the Earth's surface; also the resulting rock when cooled.

lava channel
The faster-moving, more incandescent portion of an active lava flow, or its solidified remains.

lava dome
A steep-sided mass of viscous lava, usually with a rounded top, extruded from and covering a volcanic vent.

lava flow
A stream of molten rock, usually erupted nonexplosively, that moves downslope from the vent.

lava fountain
A jet of incandescent lava sprayed from a vent by the rapid expansion of volcanic gases.

lava tube
A tunnel beneath the surface of a solidified lava flow, formed when the surface cools and subsurface molten rock keeps flowing for a time before the eruption stops or shifts, emptying the tunnel.

maar
A wide, low-relief crater formed by explosion, generally filled with water.

magma
Molten rock with dissolved gases within the Earth; magma that reaches the surface is called "lava."

magma chamber
An underground reservoir in which magma is stored.

mantle
The zone of the Earth below the crust and above the core.

mofette
Vent from which volcanic gases rich in carbon dioxide are escaping.

neck
A pipe-like vertical intrusion, usually seen as an erosional remnant of a former volcanic conduit.

obsidian
A black or dark-colored volcanic glass generally rhyolitic in composition.

oceanic ridge
A major submarine mountain range along divergent plate margins.

pahoehoe
A basaltic lava flow with a smooth, billowy, or ropy surface.

plume, mantle
A column of hot, plastic rock rising from deep within the mantle to form hotspot volcanoes.

plume, volcanic
A column or cloud of volcanic ash and gases, or of fume.

pumice
A form of volcanic glass so filled with gas bubbles and holes that it resembles a sponge and is very light.

pyroclastic deposit
The deposit of volcanic fragments from a pyroclastic flow or ashfall.

pyroclastic flow
A fluidized mass of hot rock fragments, mixed with hot gases, that moves away from a volcanic vent at high speeds.

rhyolite
A fine-grained volcanic rock with a high silica composition; similar in composition to granite.

rift system
The oceanic ridges where plates are separating and new crust is being created; also their on-land counterparts.

rift volcano
A volcano located along the rift system.

rift zone
A region of cracking and pulling apart.

Ring of Fire
The region of converging plate margins, with the resulting volcanoes and earthquakes, that surrounds the Pacific Ocean.

seafloor spreading
The aspect of plate tectonics that concerns the creation of new seafloor at the oceanic ridges as the plates separate.

shield volcano
A volcano built by flows of fluid basaltic lava, in the shape of a dome with gently sloping sides.

sinter
The siliceous deposits of hot springs, left behind when the water cools or evaporates.

skylight
In volcanology, a hole or opening in the hardened lava over an active lava tube.

solfatara
A fumarole whose gases are primarily sulfurous.

spatter cone
A cone built up around a vent by fragments of still-molten lava that weld into a solid mass.

stratovolcano
A steep volcanic cone built by both lava flows and pyroclastic deposits.

subduction zone
The zone where two tectonic plates converge, usually with one overriding the other.

travertine
Crystalline calcium carbonate deposits from hot springs.

tuff rings
The rims of explosion debris (tuff) that surround wide, shallow craters.

USGS
United States Geological Survey, the federal agency that surveys and maps the land and geological features, including volcanoes.

vent
An opening at the Earth's surface through which volcanic materials are erupted.

vog
Volcanic fog or haze caused by aerosols of volcanic gases and water.

INDEX

EPILOGUE

In the preface to this book we said there are at least 38 national parks and monuments where volcanoes are the star attractions or have major supporting roles. Just before going to press, we can now make that number at least 39. In the last few days of his term in office, President Clinton, created six new national monuments including one of volcanic origin – Kasha-Katuwe Tent Rocks in New Mexico.

This new national monument, near Santa Fe, is a six to seven square mile area of cliffs and canyons eroded into volcanic tuff and ash formations that were erupted by volcanic explosions between six and seven million years ago. These gray to beige, cone-shaped hoodoos, a few feet to 90 feet tall, look like a city of tents. Small canyons cut into the cliff faces lead into a maze of smooth and rounded walls where new hoodoos are being carved by erosion.

In our book, Kasha-KatuweTent Rocks National Monument belongs in the "Ancient Fires" category of "Hoodoos and Homesites," and indeed Native American campsites dating back as far as 7,500 years are found in the monument. The Pueblo de Cochiti, nearby, is still an inhabited settlement.

Will more volcanic areas be added to the growing list of national parks and monuments in the future? We hope so. High on our list would be the Valle Grande, the magnificent caldera just west of Los Alamos, New Mexico, and some of the beautiful volcanoes that form the Aleutian Islands. There is an old saying about the great value of beautiful land that "God's not making it anymore." With volcanoes, that's not entirely true, but the saying still justifies saving beautiful and interesting places for generations yet to come.

J.D. Griggs, USGS

MIS/126/01